THE TREACLE BUCKET

by

Elaine Dollery

Illustrated by Morag Knight

DOLLERY BOOKS

Published in Great Britain in 1992
by Dollery Books

ISBN No 0 9520252 0 5

Typeset by BP Integraphics Ltd, Bath, Avon
Printed by The Bath Press Ltd, Bath, Avon

Contents

Illustrations

Chapter 1

"Heaven is a Treacle Bucket"

Janie was a small, belligerent Shetland pony, with an addiction to black treacle, and a wicked sense of humour.

I first met her when we moved to a smallholding in Scotland, and she was living in a corner of one of the fields. She belonged to a child who had outgrown her, and she was lonely for human affection. Every day I would check her over, and give her some hay, and she would look up at me under long black lashes and maybe nip at me sideways as I passed. She was about twelve years old then as far as anyone knew, and she had more bad habits than all the other ponies put together.

It was a cold wet November when we moved in, and it rained almost non stop for three solid months. Janie's coat grew thicker and muddier, until she appeared to be covered with a matted grey brown thatch. Then came the day when she got stuck in the mud and three of us had to haul her out with ropes.

After much pulling, she finally came up like a cork out of a bottle, and stood there shaking, with the rain running in rivulets off the ends of her tangled mane. I put her into a small Shetland sized stable with a bed of thick straw and gave her a bran mash mixed up with a dollop of molasses. Janie looked at me as if heaven had descended out of that dismal winter sky. Then she closed her eyes in ecstasy and plunged her nose deep into the sticky recesses of the black bucket.

For a whole hour she stood there, steam rising in clouds from her sodden coat, while her tongue searched out every last lingering taste. Finally she decided that there was nothing left, and as I dropped some hay into her manger, she picked the empty bucket up with her teeth, and threw it at me. Straight over the low wall of the stable it sailed, and hit me bang in the middle of the chest.

That did it: I was hooked. I was in love again, with another four legged ornery beast that anyone with a grain of sense could see was not a good investment for a successful riding school.

A month later I was forty pounds poorer, and Janie was mine. When things were quiet, she was allowed to roam freely, and would wander around nibbling down the grass verges, and poking her head into the car port to see if there were any interesting titbits to be had. If the weather was bad she would put herself into her stable and snuggle down into the straw, but sometimes on very cold nights she would sleep standing up, her chin resting on the white wall of her stable, with Coka Cola the black cat curled up asleep on her back, her own personal hot water bottie.

When the better weather came, Janie came into her own. While their parents rode, small children would be taken for a slow meandering walk through the fields and back down the track, with many stops

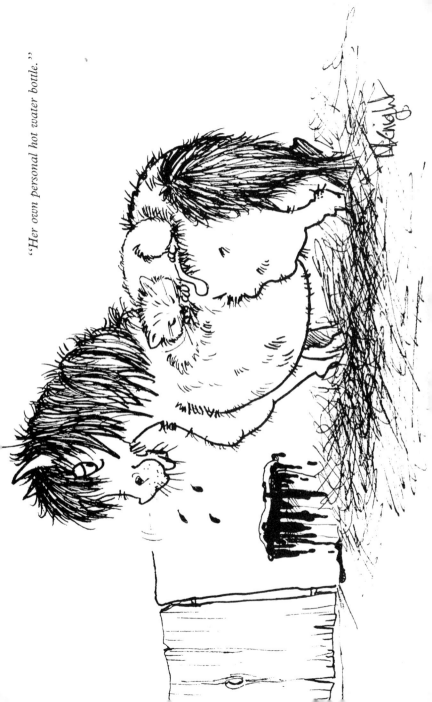

"Her own personal hot water bottle."

for "flowers for Mummy", and numerous mouth-fuls of green grass for Janie. A slow pace suited us all, though on occasion we would manage a brief trot, and we would return an hour later, happy, sun kissed and very content.

For a while Janie went out on rides with the other horses, on a lead rein, the other end of which would be attached to the rider of the lead horse. The problem was that if Janie did not approve of her lead horse or her rider, she would deliberately cause trouble. Either she would stand stock still, with her eyes shut, preferably in the middle of the road, or if her lead were sixteen hand Barona, she would place herself firmly plus rider under the larger horse's stomach, her tail and mane acting as a tickling stick to the gelding's more private parts. The worried and embarrassed expression on the larger horse's face was worth a guinea a minute, and every time the lead horse would try to sidestep, Janie would move sideways also with an angelic expression on her very hairy face.

There was one occasion when Janie, off the leading rein, was out on a ride with a seven year old girl on her back, who squealed with fright every time a car came past, or one of the horses changed step. For a time Janie stood it, and then at one particularly loud yell, she took off at full canter, with the child clinging on for dear life, still yelling at the top of her voice. Down the track Janie raced, tail streaming and nostrils flaring, until she reached the open gate to the hay field! A sharp turn, still plus squealer in the saddle, and Janie careered head-long across the field to the nearest large hay bale,

8

which was waiting to be stacked. She then stopped dead, tipping her by now breathless rider on top of the hay, closed her eyes and sunk her steaming nose deep into the fresh green hay.

Janie was a loner: she liked a quiet corner of a field, sheltered from the wind, where she could doze the days away. Occasionally she would pair up with one other horse, but as she was so small, she was liable to be bullied by the bigger ponies, and so mostly she kept herself to herself. This continued until Major arrived. To the human eye, he was very white and very old, and very small, being about 10 hands high, but in his own mind he was a dashing great stallion, destined to lead.

When he was delivered and came trotting out of the black entrance to the horse box, we put him in with Janie. His tail went up immediately, and they introduced themselves with many nose touchings, little step dances, and on Janie's part, coquettish squeals. They were happy and obviously delighted with their miniature world, and the two of them became inseparable.

On occasion, when the weather was warm, and the grass grew green and lush in the fields, Major would show us how he could jump. With very light weight riders, preferably with suction pads in their breeches, Major would fly round the jumps at twenty miles an hour, and would then retire again, panting and puffing like a baby white dragon, to be greeted by Janie with a disgusted snort or a sideways nip of affection.

Major was adept at escaping. Being so small he could wriggle under fences and through holes designed by foxes, and as anyone who has kept horses will tell you, where one horse goes, so the others follow. Once Major was through a gap, the next pony in size would slither through, enlarging the escape route as it went. This would continue, until Major would be proudly leading a group of ten delighted ponies into the nearby fields, usually at dawn, just before everyone was awake enough to realise what Houdini was up to.

Usually Janie would follow him, but if she were tired or a bit lame, she used to turn her back, snort with disgust, and then stand waiting patiently for Major's return. Lameness is a very great problem for little ponies, who will eat themselves circular on spring grass, and then suffer from laminitis, caused by too rich feeding. Once a pony has had laminitis, it will always recur and we used to spend hours, forcibly walking or dragging an unco-operative Janie to get her circulation going and her weight down. Being basically idle she could not see why she should walk and struggle around a bare field, when her hooves hurt and there were lovely lush green mouthfuls of fodder on the other side of the fence.

She was also musical: a lot of horses like trotting round or moving to music, but Janie liked it for its own sake. My daughter played flute and piano, and her room had a patio door leading onto a track by the stables. If she played the flute, all the horses would start cantering around. The piccolo would make them gallop round tossing their heads, and I always thought that the high notes made their ears ache. They certainly had that effect on mine, which was why this musical bedroom was at the back of the farm, out of general earshot. Classical piano music had no effect on the ponies, but rumpety tumpety tunes were an immediate attraction. Several would line up at the fence and listen, but Janie, my privileged mascot, would wander down the track, put her head in through the patio door, rest her whiskery chin on edge of the piano and close her eyes in bliss.

"Onward Christian Soldiers" was a great favourite, and the only way to get her to move out of the doorway was to play something highbrow, which would drive her back to the yard, in search of further amusement. Later this room was turned into a "Granny Flat", which opened up whole new possibilities for hungry Shetlands.

As she grew older Janie developed arthritis, and she was reduced to a gentle walking pace. Pensioned off from work, she used to stroll slowly around the farm, looking for titbits. Fresh mushrooms grew in abundance in September, and Janie knew where the best patches were. She also found a pony's paradise, called "Granny's Garden". With a fresh green hedge, just the right height for Shetlands, and juicy plants in little tubs, Janie thought this was Eldorado. Granny raised her fence higher and higher, until only the tip of a questing black nose could be seen over the top, while inside her jealously guarded perimeter, Granny lay in wait armed with a broom and a shriek. Eventually when the tops had been eaten off most of the little trees, a truce was called, and Janie returned to her listening post in the car port under the kitchen window.

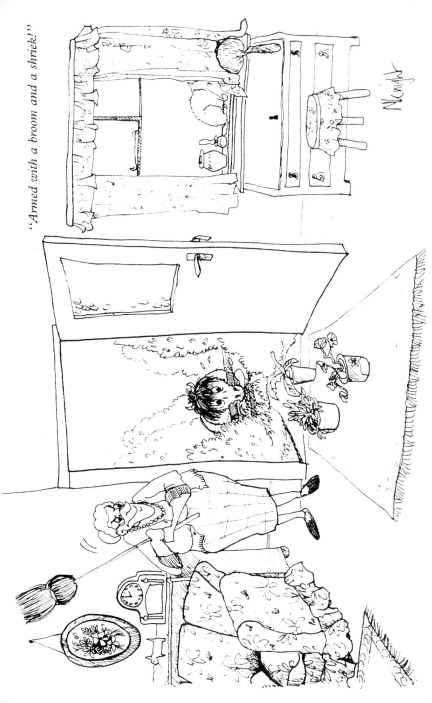

"Armed with a broom and a shriek!"

Although she was getting on in years, Janie regularly came into season at the most inconvenient times, and she was a terrible flirt, with definite ideas above her station. There was one such occasion on a warm day in June, when I was out: she had managed to unhook the rope holding the paddock gate closed and had wandered slowly across the yard over to the stables in search of entertainment or the odd forgotten pony nut. When she got there she found that the stalls were full of big beautiful geldings which were staying the night, before a nearby event being held the following day.

Janie was in heaven: she squealed, she pirouetted, she rubbed noses where she could reach them, and the steading was soon in an uproar. Hearing the squeals Granny rushed out and beat at Janie with a broom trying to drive her out of the gangway between the stalls. This had no effect, so Granny found a black bucket and poured in oats and black treacle, and held it out in front of Janie's quivering nostrils. Hypnotised with greed, Janie advanced an eager tongue, while Granny slowly retreated backwards out of the stable block where the big horses were, and enticed her into her own small stable round the corner. Once there, Janie started to lick out the bucket and Granny fastened up the door with everything she could lay hands on. She then retired back to the peace of her garden, and quiet returned to the stable block.

There is no cure for arthritis, and in the freezing white of winter, Janie would be tucked into her stable each night with Major next door, a hot bran mash laced with her beloved black treacle, and

"Janie was in heaven."

purple leg warmers on her aching legs. She loved it, and she stayed toffling around the steading and yard, and growing slower and slower, until the day when we had to leave. It was as if she knew, for I found her in the barn, unable to get up.

She must have been well over twenty by then, and I like to think that somewhere, still wandering gently around those fields, are a pair of little ghost ponies, one white and one black. I know they still wander through my heart.

Chapter 2

"The Joker"

Many horses have a sense of humour, but I found that the smaller the pony the greater its sense of mischief. Roughly speaking, ponies up to 14.2 hands seem to have a mental age of an eight year old child: often they are vulgar, usually they are funny, and most of them are lovable. Horses, above that height, are more conscious of their dignity, and often behave like moody teenagers. They have their likes and their dislikes, as people do, but they are more forthright. If they dislike another horse, they either kick it or ignore it, and you have to be careful which horses are stabled next to each other if you want a peaceful stables. Horses make friends and often pair off in the field, and they will drive other animals away from what they consider their particular patch.

A group of nine or so horses and ponies will generally settle down happily enough, provided there is enough grazing, and they are not having to compete for food. They organize their own pecking order, and the most important ones have first claim on any feed. That is why it is necessary to give them separate haynets if they are in a communal field or barn, otherwise the smallest may lose out. A gelding will normally give way to a mare, and some geldings far prefer male company in any case, but they all have different characters.

Snoopy was a joker. When I first saw him, he was in a group of horses at a dealers, and he looked sideways at me out of the corner of his long lashed eyes, asking nothing and expecting nothing. Pitch black, pot bellied and hungry looking, he just stood there accepting whatever life might throw at him, waiting. We had gone to the dealer to buy some larger ponies or horses for the riding school, and after we had tried various horses out, we came upon Snoopy.

"You need to be careful of that one," the dealer remarked. He's got a wicked streak. Not reliable for what you want."

I looked at Snoopy, and stroked him behind his ears. He rolled the whites of his eyes at me, and snuffled hopefully at the palm of my hand. His mane was long and tangly, and his coat was dull, but there was something about him.

"He can jump alright, but you'd be safer with this one." The man pointed at a grey horse standing quietly at the back. His name's Eric."

I looked at Eric, and then I returned to Snoopy. There was something about him. He had an uncared for look, and he did need feeding up. I had a sudden mental vision of him in the open field in front of the steading, where the grass swept across the valley to the hills beyond. Probably not a good buy, but when tried he seemed quiet to ride, hopped over a couple of low jumps, and stood still when a tractor engine was started up under his long nose. His conformation was bad, but he passed the vet's test as being basically a healthy animal, and so we boxed him up and brought him back to the farm.

Now when a new horse comes into a stables, it has to be quarantined in case it spreads infection. Also first and foremost it usually needs delousing, worming and grooming, and treating with extreme caution, in case it has some bad habit like refusing male riders, or biting people unexpectedly. Snoopy definitely had lice, with tell tale rough patches at the root of his mane and on his forehead, and his coat was dull and rather shaggy, but these were easy to put right. The other problems appeared later, all of which came out of the fact, that though not the most beautiful of ponies, Snoopy did not like to be laughed at, or mocked or taken for granted. He did not suffer fools gladly.

That first day, he was shampooed, an indignity which he hardly noticed, as his front end was completely occupied with a bucket of bran mash and a haynet. As the shampoo was rinsed off, a rug was put over his back with straw underneath to dry him off, and once dry he was groomed. Gradually his eyes grew brighter, and his coat began to shine. Snoopy dropped his nose into my hand and snuffled his thanks, blew hopefully at the empty bucket, and was then turned out into the green grass of the front field. From here he could see other horses, but was separated from them by the track that led from the road up to the steading.

Once in the field, he gave a couple of little jumps, turned round, rolled luxuriously for about five minutes, and then fell fast asleep instantly. For Snoopy life was good.

For two days he slept, awaking only to eat or be groomed, and after every laden bucket I carried out to him, he sang his little hymn of praise into my hand. He had obviously decided that I was his personal protector, and this is when the trouble began. The third day I went through the gate with one or two other people; Snoopy put back his ears, bared his teeth, and drove them all straight out of the field, circling round and round me as if I was his most treasured possession. It took me several long minutes to escape, and for days afterwards I had to hide round the back of the stables at feeding time, so that he couldn't see me, while everyone took a turn in feeding him, and gradually Snoopy became used to the fact that food, glorious food, arrived regularly in black buckets or haynets attached to various pairs of willing hands, and not just from me.

Once this little problem was sorted out, he began to grow sleek and with all the grooming and vitamins, his coat started to shine like polished jet. You could see your face in it. However, when not occupied with the intake of food, he did nothing but sleep, and grow fat. We found that you could go up to him as he lay flat out on the ground snoring away, sit down on the grass and lean against him and still he would sleep the sleep of the just, all day and every day. He just did not want to get up. I was worried. Most horses, when fed properly, gallop around, or dance round the fields at dawn, but not Snoopy. He slept and slept and slept.

Afraid that he might have some blood disease, I had the vet check him over, and nobody could find anything wrong whatsoever. Snoopy didn't have a problem, he just liked being asleep.

I had been well and truly taken in. From then on he was exercised and as his condition improved, so he was put to work. After some schooling, Snoopy became very useful, and very popular with some of the people who came to ride. He did however have a very uncomfortable trot, impossible to sit down to and very very bouncy. Riding him bareback was agonising, and for obvious reasons he was more suited to a woman rider than to a man. He did not really like men very much, and was most responsive to quiet, gentle riders. If someone wished him to do more than he considered right, Snoopy had his own way of dealing with them.

We first discovered this while out on a hack one day, when Snoopy had a rather heavy handed young man called Bob on his back. All was going well, and at a suitable spot the ride had a short canter. Snoopy cantered quietly along, and his canter was much more comfortable than his trot, when the man yanked on the bit. Snoopy snorted, half stopped in order to get his rider off balance, dipped his right shoulder, dropped his nose, and dumped Bob neatly on the ground. Five minutes later the remounted Bob again yanked at the reins and was again unceremoniously dumped. After that we put only light handed riders on Snoopy and warned them about Snoopy's little trick.

The odd thing was that if we took out some blind riders, as we did on special days, Snoopy always behaved himself perfectly, whatever they did, and we found that most geldings would naturally take

"Snoopy was difficult to find."

great care of any rider with either a mental or physical handicap.

On another occasion, six ponies plus six children were being given a riding lesson from a very experienced instructress, who had a rather abrasive manner. This lady spent five long minutes holding forth on Snoopy's apalling conformation, pointing out fortissimo every little bodily fault he possessed, while the six ponies trotted obediently round and round and round her, keeping close to the walls of the indoor school.

Finally she finished her damning peroration, and turned her back on him. Without even breaking step, Snoopy moved neatly sideways, dropped his shoulder and gave her a short sharp thrust between her shoulder blades. Over she went, performing two ungainly forward somersaults in the middle of the ring, while Snoopy nipped back into line and continued quietly round and round and round in perfect time with all the others. He looked a very happy pony!

We grew very fond of Snoopy in the stables. Visiting children staying at the farm were fascinated by his endless ability to sleep. Stretched out in deep straw, he would appear dead, except for an occasional twitch of an ear, if a fly disturbed his slumber, and he always slept flat out on his side, in a state of soporific bliss, with the rotund curve of his stomach rising solidly above him. Snoopy never stood up if he could lie down, and he never lay down without falling fast asleep. You could sit on top of him, tickle him, or lean against his back and snooze yourself; he would never stir.

In long grass of course, this made it difficult to find him, but getting him awake and on his feet was harder still. It took a bridle, a rope, a large vocabulary and great determination to rouse him, but he was otherwise very amenable, and when his eyes finally opened , he would be very pleased to see you.

Like all the horses, he had his admirers and eventually he went to live on a smallholding, where he was, and still is "spoilt rotten". For Snoopy, life is good.

Chapter 3

"Trot on, Tommy"

One evening we had a frantic phone call from a lady living a couple of miles away. She was looking after a house and garden for a friend, and a foal had just been delivered, and had broken out of the shed in which he had been placed by the carrier.

"Please can you help? There are sheets of glass against the wall, and I'm afraid he going to cut himself to shreds, and I can't catch him."

My daughter and the groom, Angie, grabbed ropes and halters, and I drove them along to the house where the foal, which had been nicknamed "Tommy", was rushing around the lawn and having a high old time. By the time he was finally attached to a halter and two lead ropes, it was dark, and I drove slowly ahead to light the way, and warn oncoming traffic. Cries of "Trot on Tommy" echoed behind me, and were repeated ad lib for the next hour, while the tired foal walked and trotted along the roads and tracks towards the farm. "Trot on Tommy" echoed through the night air, as he halted for a reviving bite of grass and a brief restorative drink at a stream, and by the time he reached the steading, he was well and truly halter broken and a very sleepy little foal.

Let loose in a large stable full of straw, he dropped his eyelids, his knees folded and he was out for the count before he hit the bedding. There he remained fast asleep until sun up next day.

The following morning the absent owner rang and came over to collect him.

"I don't know what the fuss was all about: he could have easily been turned loose in the field next to the house," she said. We looked at each other sheepishly.

"We didn't know a field was there and it was getting dark," we said. "Sorry about that!"

"Not your fault," she replied. "I'm only glad he's alright."

We led the foal out, and he walked meekly out of the stable complete with halter and lead rope. We were sorry to see him go: with his long knobbly legs and liquid brown eyes he was quite enchanting. By now he is a full grown pony with probably a different name altogether, but we shall always remember him as "Trot on Tommy!"

All young animals are attractive, and horses are very gentle towards foals, partly I think because they are never quite sure whose "children" they are! We had three foals born at the farm while we were there, and I used to spend hours just watching them. Their dam was a part Arab mare, very dainty, called Amber, who used to float as she cantered. That is one of the lovely things about Arabs: at times as they move they seem to hover between earth and heaven.

I remember one occasion up in Fife, going to

see a mare at one of the hill farms. It was dusk when we arrived, as we had as usual become lost on the way, and the moor rose up dark against the evening sky. The farmer wandered out from the steading and whistled twice, and over the brow of the hill, manes flowing and tails streaming black against the red of the sunset, a group of five Arabs galloped headlong, their hooves thundering against the ground. Silhouetted against the fading light, they seemed to float in the air. I was in love yet again, exhilarated and enchanted, and not a little afraid as they charged down towards us, in case I was going to be trampled into the mud. We didn't buy an Arab that time; we couldn't afford it, and they are not really suitable for riding stables, as they are too fiery, but it was a near thing.

In the borders, I have seen two hundred horses galloping as one, and I have watched the herds of ponies on Dartmoor and Exmoor, and those that graze wild and free on the Welsh hillsides, but nothing for me has ever matched the wild beauty of the Arabs. Indeed, when we started up the stables, I wanted all grey horses, preferably Arabs, but they do not make quiet hacks, and as any groom will tell you, white horses are very difficult to keep clean. Hence the Janies and the Snoopies and the Trot on Tommies that came into our lives.

Geldings are the most practical horses for a riding stables, as they are calmer than mares, who become distinctly flighty when in season, which occurs yearly at intervals from March until

September. Geldings are never quite sure about mares, who seem remarkably fickle in their affections, and will pal up with one bedazzled gelding for a while, and then drop the poor chap dead if a more handsome suitor comes along.

When our first foal was born into the bright morning light of a May dawn, we missed the birth by five minutes, arriving just in time to see the afterbirth fall. The foal, golden chestnut against the green grass of the field, lay in a heap, its mother licking ecstatically at its damp head and body.

In a few minutes the foal tried to stand up; its legs buckled and it fell upon its nose. Again and again it tried, and each time one or other of its legs would give way. To co-ordinate four at once seemed an impossibility, and when it finally achieved this, it quivered from head to tail with the effort, while Amber gave litttle whickers and snorts of encouragement. Then began the search for the milk bar which nature so bountifully provides. The problem was that as this was a first foal and very new to the big wide world, neither mother nor daughter knew how to locate the udder. It was a very anxious half hour before contact was finally made, and loud ecstatic suckling noises were heard as the foal absorbed the milky colostrum which would keep it alive. Its frizzled little tail whisked happily from side to side like a lamb's, and Mother and foal were united in their own personal heaven.

We could have watched all day, and we were not the only spectators. Amber and foal, whom we christened Chrystal, were in a paddock edged on two of its sides by fields where the geldings grazed. Every single one was pressed up as close to the fence as he could get, eyes popping, mouth half open, and every single one seemed to be saying:

"Is it mine, Amber, Oh! is it mine?"

As Chrystal grew bigger, she became very friendly with our rough collie, Bumble. Maybe it was because Chrystal was chestnut with one white foot, and Bumble was golden with a thick white ruff, and not much more than a puppy herself, but the two of them used to play tig round and round the field, with the foal prancing from side to side, and pretending to chase the dog, who in turn would crouch down with her nose resting on her front paws, only to leap up into the air, and then the two of them would career in circles like mad things, drunk with the sheer joy of being alive.

Meanwhile Amber would trot round after them, with the worried expression of a mother whose toddler has strayed too far, and this would go on until all three would suddenly stand quite still, the milk bar would open, and after a feed, the foal would fall contentedly asleep with a tummy full of warm milk, and the sun on its back. Amber would stand over it, half dozing, with a watchful eye out for any danger, while Bumble curled up contentedly near by, waiting for her playmate to wake up again.

The very young have no fear. Provided the dam will let you near, you can handle a foal, stroke it and get a foal slip over its head as soon as it is

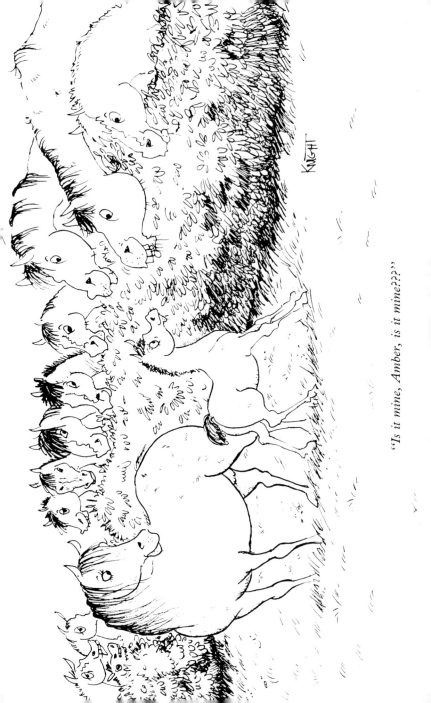

"Is it mine, Amber, is it mine???"

born. A slip is a miniature head collar, made usually of soft leather, with a small tail or rope hanging down under the chin. The idea is that you get hold of this and lead the foal around. The trouble is that within a few days, the dam teaches the foal to keep away from visitors, and gets possessively between you and the foal whenever you approach, driving it away from you in ever widening circles, so that if you don't manage to get the slip on right at the beginning, you will find it very difficult to do so later.

In the same way, a bitch will guard her puppies, and even good tempered dogs can become extremely tetchy if they think their young are being handled too much. Most animals are the same. Once out on the forest in Wales my husband found a newborn deer half hidden in the undergrowth. It was completely fearless and obviously thought that our Collie Bumble was its Mother, because it rushed up to her and tried to suckle. They spent an enchanted hour up there with it, and had great difficulty in persuading it not to follow them. Later he went up to check that it was alright, and found it gone, so the Mother must have come back to collect it. If it had been day or two older, it would have lain hidden and unmoving until its dam returned.

One of the grooms at the farm once found a leveret out in the field where its Mother had left it. It lay as if frozen, completely still and she only saw it because she was building jumps, and it was hidden between a couple of poles lying on the ground. Even when discovered it played dead, and she crept away, and built the jumps somewhere else. When she went back an hour later there was no sign of it, apart from a small hollow in the grass, and it was never left there again. In Spring we often saw hares racing across the fields. Completely oblivious of us, traffic or danger, they would run in front of the cars, stop suddenly and leap straight up into the air, jumping over each other or just dancing alone full of the sheer delight of being alive.

Chapter 4

"The Schoolmaster"

White horses, or greys as they are called, were always my favourites. Major was the smallest we acquired, but one size up at 13.2 hands high came Misty. Snowy white and twelve years old when we bought him, he was a Welsh Mountain pony and a schoolmaster. Misty knew it all: gymkhanas were his happy hunting ground, and he was very gentle with children, but he had his faults. Firstly, he used to pull the most awful faces, wrinkling up his nose, and baring his teeth, with his lips curled right back, so that he appeared very fierce; secondly he would not be caught.

It took us three weeks to figure out how to catch him in the field. Inevitably he would let you get within a yard, take the piece of carrot out of your outstretched hand and with a flick of his heels he would be off to the far end of the paddock. There he would stop, drop his head and graze peacefully, while you trudged patiently after him, lead rope hidden behind your back, staring up at the sky, the other horses or the view, and pretending all the while that the last thing in the world you wanted to do was to get anywhere near an obstinate little white pony. Misty used to enjoy this and obviously he thought it was a marvellous game, especially designed to exercise humans and to make them jump up and down with frustrated rage. Sometimes he would dash towards you as if he were going to attack, only to rear up and wheel away at the last minute. He would curl his top lip right back and sneer at you, but he never actually harmed anyone: it was all show. Occasionally I swear he gave a horse laugh.

We must have walked miles trying to catch him. We tried carrots, pony nuts, sweet smelling black buckets full of steaming bran mash: none of these worked and even black treacle had no effect. Misty knew every trick in the book, and was not to be fooled. As a spectator sport it was a fine form of exercise, but when you were rushed for time, and trying to catch, feed, groom and saddle up fourteen assorted horses and ponies it was infuriating. In the end we used to catch all the other horses and ponies first, and would then try to encircle Misty with long ropes and as many helpers as possible. When finally cornered he used to heave a little sigh, pull another terrible face and stand quietly while you dropped a halter over his head. There was no malice in him, but he did not like being caught. I always thought that perhaps when he was younger, he had been hit for running away, and that this had taught him to keep as far as possible from people in general.

Finally one day quite by chance we cracked it. As usual we had brought all the other horses in and given them feeds, and the gate to the field had been left open, with Misty skulking in the furthest corner. Suddenly he gave a loud whinny, hurled himself into full gallop and charged straight for the

"Misty knew every trick in the book."

gate, wheeled through it, turned sharply into the stables, and slid to a halt in his usual place. We couldn't believe it. All that chasing, walking, swearing and frustration had been for nothing. Misty just did not like being alone without other horses to talk to, and he didn't like being caught in the open. After that we never tried to catch him; instead we left him to find his own way through open gates to his awaiting feed bucket, and he used to come in like a little white lamb.

Most horses are sociable, and their herd instinct is strong. Usually, if you left a field gate open, first one horse would wander out and then another would follow, until finally the whole maddening herd would be careering down the track, heading for freedom, with grooms, riders and me, haring diagonally across the front field to head them off before they reached the road. An entrance track of half a mile or more is a definite plus where there are possible escapers. If a new horse is added to a herd, it may well decide to jump out and go and find its original companions, so it is necessary to keep a wary eye on any newcomers, and to keep gates firmly shut. Misty however was a law unto himself: he didn't want to run away; all he wanted was to stay with the others and to organise his own life.

Misty liked equine company, and one frosty morning at first light I was looking out over the front field, where we had nine assorted horses and ponies. They all looked very peaceful: most of them were asleep standing up, with their heads low, and their warm breath puffing out in little white clouds. Snoopy of course was lying down asleep, with his outstretched head resting on the remnants of last night's hay.

The only sound was the distant barking of a dog, and the calling of a skein of wild geese flying overhead. My heart leaped with sudden happiness as I heard them. I felt as if I too were flying free, winging my way to distant places, at one with the wind and the dawn fresh sky. At the sound, Misty stirred and threw up his head. Then he stretched first forwards with his nose to his hooves, and then luxuriously backwards with his hind legs extended as far as they would go. Then he looked around him at the other horses, and with little mincing steps he walked over to Janie, and touched her nose with his, which made her snort. Next he dropped his head right down to the ground with his legs straight out in front, and reared up in a little pirouette, tossing his white mane as he rose. Janie gave a start, and swung her rump round as if to kick, but Misty was gone, trotting over to the next horse. Again he dropped his nose to the ground, touched noses and rose up on his hind legs, and the next horse was awake, and doing the same. Up reared each horse in turn opposite Misty as if taking part in a formal dance. Round and round went the little white schoolmaster, touching each horse in turn like a whirling alarm clock, until he had the whole herd wide awake and racing round the field, flying free with the wild geese at the dawning of the day.

This routine happened many times, and I never tired of watching, and always it was Misty who started the waking ritual. If he was not there, the horses would wake up individually, and the morning choral dance would not take place.

Other animals came into the front field. Deer would skirt the edges, and a fox would follow the same path each morning, passing close to the derelict hen house by the stream. Herons would fly up from the river and drift silently down to the water, where they would stand for hours, one legged and watchful. There were two young ones, the edges of their wings grey tipped, and one the great grand daddy of them all, whose wings were edged with great black pinions, and whose wing span must have been a good six feet. They always hunted singly, and each had their own stretch of stream where they would fish undisturbed.

In wet weather, great clouds of water birds, gulls and crows would descend , but the odd thing was that they operated a system of apartheid. If you had a mass of white gulls strutting about one side of the paddock, all the crows and other black coloured birds would remain on the other side, as if refusing to acknowledge the presence of the others, while many coloured or dun coloured birds would roam around and mingle freely in their search for the tasty worms that came up to the surface after the rain.

Once a goose caused a complete power cut which lasted for hours. This was because the electricity line to the farm was single phase and ran from the road and across three neighbouring fields, and one wild and windy day just before harvest, we saw a bird flying low before the wind and crashing with a great blue flash into the electricity line. I rang the electricity board, telling them where the line was down, and that the barley was sizzling, and they came out very swiftly to repair it, while I fed the household on cold baked beans and sardines. The children thought this was a delicious meal, and just as I had potatoes ready and baking in the fire, the power came on again, and the friendly world of candles and shadows vanished in a blaze of electric light. This happened soon after we moved to the farm, and afterwards when we realised how frequent power cuts were, we kept a good store of candles, torches, and little camping cookers, together with a selection of safety lanterns for use in the stables.

In winter when most of the horses would be bedded down, or turned into the indoor school for shelter during the night, those that were out in the fields would be rugged up or left long coated for warmth. One of the most satisfying times was when you could wander round the stables on a final evening check: each horse would be contentedly chewing hay or dozing, and would greet you with little whinnies and whickers and maybe a soft nose dropping into your hand over the stable door.

In summer most of the horses would be out in the fields, and when their daily work was done each of the ponies had their own way of relaxing. Misty would trot into the field, bend his head down and shake himself vigorously, ending with a final fling of his mane. Then he would lie down and roll slowly from side to side to get the itches out of his back, with his four legs waving in ridiculous fashion above his extended stomach. Finally he would stand up, gaze all around him, and wander off to the particular patch of grass that he knew awaited him.

Horses like to live by a set time-table, with food, work and relaxation happening at regular intervals. If their feeds are late, they get very upset, and will start squabbling or grumbling among themselves. Once a routine is established, and the horse knows what to expect and what is expected of him in return for food and shelter, there will be very little trouble. It is only when everything seems strange and new, and an animal does not know whether its owner can be trusted that accidents occur. Not all horse owners are kind, and many are ignorant, so that a horse who has changed hands several times will become increasingly wary when it arrives in a new stables. There are very few horses that will not respond to regular feeds and kindness with a certain amount of discipline thrown in. Like people, they have different characters, and it is important to get to know them and their individual ways, so that you can work together in some sort of harmony. Like Misty, you need to be a schoolmaster.

Chapter 5

"The Escaper"

The most peripatetic horse we had was called Warren, and he was given to me on condition that I looked after small Major for as long as he lived. He was dapple grey, about fourteen hands and a very good jumper. However he had been gelded late and was firmly convinced in his own mind that he was a stallion, and as such it was his duty to round up all the mares in the vicinity.

No matter which paddock you put him into at night, first thing in the morning he would leap lightly from field to field, jumping the fences as if they were not even there, and would go and call on every mare in turn. His social duty done, he would then jump out of the final field, and come and bang at the kitchen window for breakfast. First freedom, then the mares, and then food: those were Warren's priorities, in that order.

We slept on the ground floor, and occasionally Warren would come and bang on the bedroom window in the middle of the night. This meant that some of the ponies had broken out and needed rounding up. We would then hurtle out of bed, torches in hand, in a crazy fashion parade of pyjamas, green wellies and battered anoraks to do a head count of Warren and his night walkers. These were the few occasions when people agreed with me that white horses were best, as at least they showed up in the dark, whereas you could fall headlong over a black coated Snoopy or Janie before you knew they were anywhere near.

Warren hated being shut in. Before he came to us, his owners had tried everything they could think of to contain him, as it is most unsettling to find your horse in a different field every morning, especially when the field does not belong to you. Faced with ever higher retaining fences, he just jumped higher and higher, until faced by a deer fence seven feet high.

For three weeks he was well and truly stumped, or so they thought. Then they found him out yet again, and the deer fence intact. On closer inspection, they discovered a pony sized hole beneath the wire. As the fence was too high to leap, Warren had done the other thing and dug his way out.

Only a securely locked stable could hold him, as if he could reach the bolts with his lips, he would draw them back, and not only escape himself, but would release a particular friend from another stable to keep him company, and he was also capable of clearing a five foot stable door from a standing start. The first time he did this he landed in the gangway and cut his lip on a door bolt. Out came the vet, and sewed him up, while Warren stood there sheepishly, and you could see him working out how on earth he was going to get out the next time.

Away went the vet, leaving behind a packet of disinfectant, and an overlooked twitch in the

"The night walker."

corner of the stable. Nobody likes seeing a twitch used on a horse, but it is necessary at times, and it has the advantage of almost anaesthetising an animal without the use of drugs. A twitch consists of a wooden bar about eighteen inches long, with a loop of strong fine rope attached to the curved end. The rope is twisted round the horses sensitive nose, and as it is tightened, the horse goes dopey, and ceases to feel pain, so that minor operations can be done swiftly without causing the animal distress. Once the twitch is removed, the horse just shakes its head and returns to normal, and in expert hands, a wound can be sewn up, or a cyst removed almost before the horse is aware of it. Warren was certainly unperturbed.

That same evening we put a set of bars across above the lower half door, and fastened them securely in place with ropes, so that there was no way he could leap, climb or clamber out of the stall. Defeated at last, Warren heaved a deep sigh and settled down, but he always kept a weather eye on his exit route, and woe betide anyone who left the bars unfastened as he would be out in the twinkling of an eye.

Warren had to have another minor operation quite soon after he arrived, as he had a lump under his skin. It was small, about an inch long like an elongated marble, and it first appeared on his neck high up near his withers. It didn't worry him at all, so we left it, only to find one morning that it had vanished, and was now at the top of his chest. Examining him closely we found that whatever this lump was, it was like its wearer, peripatetic, and had made itself a channel, so that it could be slid under the skin from his withers down to his chest, up the other side, and over to the centre of his back by the spine.

This was more serious, as if it lodged itself under a saddle, it could cause pain or an accident, so again out came our friendly vet. By the time he arrived, the lump was again in the middle of Warren's chest.

"Never seen anything like it," he said cheerfully, and proceeded to slide the lump back up onto Warrens' neck. A quick application of anaesthetic, and a second later the lump shot up into the air, bounced off the roof of the stable, and was caught by the vet with a shriek of laughter and a very neat right hander.

"Whatever is it," I asked, as we peered down at what looked exactly like a large dull green broad bean.

"Harmless anyway," came the reply, "It could have been caused by a horse fly bite that encapsulated, but it's unusual to say the least. You should have no further trouble." And away he went, leaving behind another twitch to keep the first one company.

After this Warren was good as gold, apart from the time when the show jumpers were staying for a couple of nights, and we had to move him out of his normal stable. The trouble was that the riders left their carefully prepared buckets of feed outside the doors of their stalls, and Warren, after undoing the bolts on his temporary habitation, had a field day devouring every delicious helping of oats in sight. I came out to find him galloping round and round like a race horse, and jumping over every fence he could find. He was uncatchable for a while, so we left him doing circuit training, and just watched until he paused for breath.

Once he had run off his surplus food, he was quite amenable, but it took him three days on hay alone, before he returned to his normal cheerful self.

Little ponies do not need oats at all, unless they are going in for marathons or expected to do a great deal of work. Roughly speaking, a race horse needs rich feeds, with lots of oats and additives to boost its energy, and is the equivalent to an aeroplane running on high octane aviation fuel. A pony going for a quiet hack, needs hay, and maybe a small feed of bran and pony nuts as a reward on its return, although if you wish to keep a horse docile, and just wish to meander gently about the countryside, unlimited hay or good grass will keep it ticking over nicely, with carrots and vitamins and a salt lick to keep it happy and in condition. Briefly to horses more feed means more bounce, and the least energising feed is hay, then on a rising scale pony nuts and grass nuts, with bran for ballast, then barley, maize and finally oats.

New grass in April can send all horses high as kites, and if it is lush, can give little ponies laminitis, as they will eat themselves circular if they are allowed to do so. This increases their weight so much that their hooves become turgid and sore and their feet swell inside the rigid casing of horn, and they go lame. They then lie down and refuse to walk

45

because of the pain, and so get fatter and fatter, and lamer and lamer. The cure is to make them walk and semi starve them back into condition, but every Spring is a risk to greedy little ponies, and once incurred laminitis can become chronic. Over-feeding is as dangerous as underfeeding, and you have to learn what each horse can digest, and what their particular metabolism needs to do the amount of work you want them to do. Overfeeding makes them unmanageable, as this next story shows.

There was once a mare in training at a stables, and despite being fed only hay, she became wilder and scattier with each passing day. Finally in des-peration, the grooms kept a secret watch on what she did, and they found that no sooner was the mare alone in her stable, than she went over to the corner and started shaking and banging against a down pipe from the loft above. As a reward down into the manger came showers of loose oats, like manna from heaven. The result of course, was one mental mare, who was most displeased when her stable was changed and her source of high octane food was cut off.

Horses are very clever at times, and their instinct is to eat everything in sight, and if there is a bucket or greener pasture nearby, they will use their natural cunning to reach it. Big horses will usually jump fences, or like Warren burrow beneath, but little ponies use other methods. Janie for example had a simple way of getting from one field to another. Either she leant heavily against a fence until it bent over, or she lay down and rolled under-neath, folding her front legs into her chest as she

"The grass is greener on the other side."

went. Major, who had obviously been Warren's original mentor, used to go down to the stream and duck under the bottom wire below the water, and get into the adjoining paddock that way. To a grazing animal the grass is always greener on the other side.

The odd thing about some horses is that though they will, like our Escaper, jump out of their field, and will happily hop over jumps for you in the paddock, the minute they are in a show ring, they go on strike. Warren was one of these. He loathed big crowds, noisy people and most of all he hated competing in public. To him jumping was necessary to get where he wanted to go, but he could see no point at all in jumping over little fences in a ring with lots of people looking at him. If he were out on a trek, he would leap a tree trunk or any obstacle in his way, because it made sense to him, but show jumping for him was an agony, and it took a very strong rider indeed to make him perform.

Another horse which we bought in called Danny, was the exact opposite. He had no interest at all in normal hacking, or pottering around at the farm. He only came alive in the show ring, and as soon as the horse box appeared and he was plaited up and groomed he was happy. It all depends on a horse's early training, and Danny, who was very handsome and difficult to handle, loathed being in the riding stables, and eventually went to live in the borders, where for a while he was running free in four hundred acres, and his owner was having enormous difficulty in catching him. Like Warren, he had escaped.

Chapter 6

"Early days"

When we first moved up to Scotland we lived in an old hall on the outskirts of a town, and we travelled up from Yorkshire in a Range Rover, which some-one had kindly leant us for the journey. Behind it we towed a bright blue horse box containing two horses: my elder daughter's Arab Prince, and my younger daughter's little black mare called Bonny. Following us and at times bypassing our erratic progress, came a furniture van, containing among other necessities, thirty six packing cases of books. Lying in the back of the enormous car lay two dogs, one cat, and both daughters, one of whom was covered with chicken pox, which had chosen to develop that very morning.

Despite our impeccable organisation, it was not an auspicious start. Within a fortnight, Bonny had a nasty cough, and Prince had lots of little cuts from sliding down the river bank. This necessitated our first call to our friendly vet, who came out and danced round and round Prince, with a can of purple antiseptic spray in his hand. Prince was grey, and with purple blotches all over his cuts looked like an advertisement for bubonic plague, and a good match for his owner, who seemed to have more chickenpox spots than anyone I had ever seen.

At that time we knew very little about ponies, and we were learning by trial and error, with lots of advice from neighbours, our helpful vet, and friendly farmers. Although I had been round horses and dogs all my life, I had never before looked after two single handed, as this was the first time we had had a suitable paddock, and my daughters, aged twelve and thirteen knew even less than I did, and we got into some rare old muddles.

For instance there was the question of grooming, and Bonny, who was very pretty, and completely black, had a very long mane and tail, which needed a great deal of attention. Imagine my horror one morning when I went out to find that Bonny had a new haircut, complete with a lopsided fringe cut high up on her forehead, and side bobs to match. She looked like a cartoon pony.

Luckily the mane grew again, and Bonny soon made good use of it to escape from her paddock. The fences were in very bad condition, and in desperation we had put up an electric fence to keep her in. Prince was easy to contain: all you had to do was to lay a long green garden hose in front of him and he would not dare to step over it. The poor horse was firmly convinced that all hoses were snakes, and he would shudder away to the opposite end of the field whenever any kind of piping appeared. Not so small Bonny. To her hose pipes were for playing with, and wires were a challenge. She used to charge headlong towards the electric fence, turn sideways at the last moment, using her heavy mane as insulation as she broke through, and away she would tear into the night.

"Bubonic plague."

The first time this happened, we were woken up by frantic bellows from Prince, who couldn't stand his lady friend disappearing, but was much too sensible to escape himself. We hurtled after her into the dark waving torches about and shouting, and suddenly Bonny shot past us and back to the paddock as fast as she had left it. After this had happened once or twice, we didn't bother to chase after her, as she invariably returned of her own accord.

We were lucky to have a large beamed shed for the two horses at the back of the farm next door, and we divided this into two stables with straw bales. Every winter night we put them in separate apartments, and every morning we would find Bonny in with Prince. Eventually we got around to putting up a proper partition, and life became easier. The trouble with having two horses in one stable is that not only do they squabble over hay, but they may kick each other. Also they can get cast. That is they can roll over in the straw and get trapped against a wall or in a corner, and in thrashing around to get up again they can sometimes damage themselves quite badly.

Bonny had no fear of anything, and was full of curiosity about everything. The day we hired a J.C.B. complete with extra large bucket to remodel part of the paddock, Prince galloped off into the overgrown walled garden, but Bonny not only kept getting in the way, she actually climbed into the bucket and started sniffing round for something to eat. Obviously she thought it was a giant sized feeding trough, and was not at all pleased when forcibly removed.

The trouble with bad fencing is that not only can your own animals escape, but others can invade your territory, and sometimes we had unexpected visitors. One Christmas morning, I woke to find a white world of frost, and thirty bullocks playing "Chase me Charlie" on the front lawn. They had escaped from the next door farm, and it was some time before I could get hold of their owner and entice them back where they belonged. A few weeks later, the temperature dropped even lower, and the steading next door which housed the cattle froze up completely, and we were running hot water through hoses across the back field in order to water the bullocks before they went crazy with thirst. We had to run hot water through, as cold froze before it reached the troughs, and we soon learnt to live in temperatures much colder than we had been used to in Yorkshire.

Our water supply arrived via a partially buried black pipe across some waste land, and we were for ever digging it out, or repairing leaks. We became expert at thawing frozen joints out underneath floorboards by using hairdryers, and in very cold weather, I would have to go to the back regions of the hall, armed with a kettle of boiling water, and supported by both dogs and a cat to ward off any mice. Once there I had to climb through a trap door and over some rafters to reach the intake valve on the water tank, which invariably froze up whenever it was more than four degrees below.

The country is beautiful in very cold weather in Scotland and sometimes I felt as if I was living inside a giant snowflake. The bare branches of the trees stood out like wrought iron against the grey sky, and the frost on the hedges looked like delicate filigree lace. The whole world would be in differing shades of grey, white and black, and any sound was amplified by the piercing cold. At minus fifteen the very air seemed to sparkle as you breathed out, and the ice particles glittered like crushed diamonds under the winter sun.

Snow was a different matter. As it melted the roof leaked in various places, and we would stuff plastic bags into holes in the high roof of the main building, or my daughters would climb up and replace loose tiles on the single story extension at the rear. In summer there was a wild bees nest in the attic below the roof joists, so temporary repairs then were distinctly hazardous. As far as unexpected visitors went we definitely preferred the bullocks.

The bees soon expanded their territory, and caused a great deal of trouble. It happened like this. One autumn afternoon I was inside the house and the children were playing outside in the paddock. It was a fine day, but windy, and the windows were beginning to rattle. After one gust, I suddenly felt unreasoning panic, and rushed outside yelling for the children to come inside immediately. They were not amused, as they were quite happy in the paddock with Prince and Bonny, and the hall and outbuildings sheltered them from the worst of the wind. However I hauled them inside, and ten seconds later there was a crack of thunder, a roar of wind, and a terrific crash, followed by a groaning and a grinding noise from the paddock. The old elm tree which had been growing in the field for two hundred years or so, had split in two. Half remained leaning over the back of the house, and the other half lay stretched out across the paddock in a tangle of broken branches just where the children had been playing. Prince was in the far corner shaking all over with fright, with Bonny for once hiding behind him.

As we stood there looking at the fallen giant, there was a scream of brakes, and several cars appeared. The sound of the crashing tree had reached the nearby estate, and all the men working there had rushed down to see if we needed rescuing, and were all prepared for the worst. It was obviously an anti climax to find that no-one had been hurt, and it took a while to convince them that we were perfectly well and just standing there, unsquashed and counting our blessings.

The next problem was the half tree overhanging the house and the power lines. It is not easy to get tree fellers out in a storm, and the wind was getting up to gale force, and it was cold. After much telephoning two men appeared and one volunteered to climb up and take down the overhang. He went up swiftly complete with ropes, and having fastened himself to the trunk for safety, he braced his feet against the trunk and started up the electric saw. As the blade bit into the wood with a whine, there was a furious buzzing and out swarmed a dozen or so wild bees, annoyed by the disturbance of their nest, which had been hidden in a hollow just where the great tree had split. The tree feller came down faster than he had gone up, and we stood below and watched the angry black specks whirling up above us, determined to defend their territory from invaders.

It is not easy to get bee experts out in a storm, and after more telephone calls it was agreed to leave the whole thing until the next morning, when the storm should have blown itself out. By ten oclock the following day there were six cars of spectators, the post man, the man from the electricity board who had come to read the meter, and several visitors whom I had never seen before. Everyone was very cheerful; a few bets were made privately concerning bees, trees and power lines and I made several pots of tea. Half an hour later out came a bee expert complete with smoke gun, and our tree feller, together with the tools of his trade. These included a large tractor, chains and ropes, and some heavyweight men. By the time the ropes and chains had been attached to the tree and the tractor, and the bees smoked into temporary compliance, everyone was having a high old time. The number of visiting cars had increased to eight, and I was running out of teabags.

Finally came the moment for which everyone had been waiting. The overhanging half of the elm was partly severed and the tractor started up. For about ten seconds nothing happened, and then there was a sharp crack as the trunk swung ominously towards the house. The tractor crunched forward over the broken twigs and leaves that strewed the ground and all the heavyweight men leaned into their ropes. Slowly the trunk swayed round and crashed on top of the fallen branches. A cloud of dust rose and a few sleepy bees flew drunkenly out of the broken shards of trunk. Everyone heaved a sigh of relief, and slowly the crowd dispersed back to the business of getting on in this modern world, while the two hundred year giant lay shattered at my feet.

It is no good being sentimental about fallen trees, but I felt very small and very lucky as I stood there, and very grateful for all the help people had given. I also gave up a small prayer of thankfulness for the warning that had sent me helter skelter out into the paddock to retrieve my children from the path of the rising wind.

Chapter 7

"Of Owls & Pussy Cats"

The Hall paddock ran alongside a railway line, beyond which lay a small salmon river, and when we first moved in Prince was scared stiff of the trains, and would gallop away in fright every time one clattered by. Bonny remained unperturbed and by the end of the first fortnight Prince had become used to the sudden noise and would stay where he was and throw up his head to look as the carriages came past. Another week and he ignored the trains completely.

A month or so later I rode Prince out of the dilapidated gate, through the farm building behind and down a track towards the railway. The small road led between rising banks covered with bushes, and there on an elder branch at the edge of the track perched a sleepy looking barn owl. It was so close to me that if I had stretched out my hand I could have touched it, but it was completely unafraid. I must have sat there quietly watching it for about twenty minutes, and it gazed back at me out of its huge dark eyes, unblinking in its white face. I had seen owls swooping at dusk, but never so close or in daylight, and I was fascinated. If I had been on foot, it would have flown away at my approach, but for some reason if you are riding peacefully about the countryside, wild animals regard you as part of the horse, and seem to have no fear.

Eventually I walked on and the owl's head swivelled as I left and headed for the arch under the railway. I had been so absorbed in bird watching, and it was such a quiet warm sleepy afternoon, that I was not really paying attention to my surroundings, and just as I reached the exact centre of the railway arch, there was a devastating roar, and a train charged overhead, rattling the bridge supports and frightening the living daylights out of both me and my horse.

Prince took off at full gallop straight towards the river bank, and I only just managed to cling on and swing him back onto the muddy track that lay parallel to the railway line. On roared the train and on galloped Prince, with me bent low over the saddle and hanging on for dear life. After a hundred yards the road veered left over the river and we clattered over the wooden bridge leaving the train behind. It took another hundred yards before Prince ground to a halt, and I slid shaking off his back. Riding is not my strong point, and it was years since I had been on a bolting horse. After that I used to listen very carefully if I went riding in that direction, and would make a dash through the railway arch in between train times.

There were a lot of owls round the hall, living in barns or hollow trees, and we used to hear them hunting as night fell. If you imitated their call, they would answer you thinking you were another owl, and come looking to see who was invading their territory.

In old houses you get all sorts of creaks and odd

noises at night, and for a few days we had been hearing scritchety scratchety sounds coming from the blocked up fireplace in our bedroom. I thought it was starlings nesting in the chimney, as often happens, and had removed the cover to see if any birds were trapped behind. However, it was not until we were having dinner one night that we discovered what our visitor was. The children, who were supposed to be asleep, rushed into the sitting room full of excitement.

"Mummy, come quick, there's an owl in the bedroom and it's flying round and round."

"Rubbish: I don't believe you. Go back to bed," I replied thinking this was just an excuse to come downstairs.

"No, honestly, come and see quickly," and they dragged us out of the door and up the stairs, followed by our dinner guests.

Sure enough in the middle of the bedroom ceiling, perched on the chandelier, was a young tawny owl. It was very small, about thirty centimetres high, and with its fluffy brown feathers and its large brown eyes, it looked like a little old college professor, benignly surveying his latest intake of students. As we moved round the room, its head turned right round with us, swivelling on its brown feathered shoulders, as if on a hinge. It was not afraid of us, until we tried to catch it, which took about five minutes. The children drew back the heavy curtains and opened a window, and cradling it gently between my hands, where it felt as light as air, I tossed it out into the night. With a whir of wings it was gone.

Tawny owls are rarely seen in daylight, as they usually spend their days in hollows in trees, and if found outside, are often mobbed by other birds until they take refuge in the nearest hole. In this case the nearest refuge must have been our unused chimney.

Other regular visitors were foxes, which kept their distance, and wild cats, which didn't. The true wild cat is supposed to be tabby, slightly larger than the domesticated animal, and with more pronounced markings. Then there are cross breeds, where the two have interbred, and the kittens are untameable, and domestic cats which have taken to the wild, and which live on their wits without the aid of man.

Some time after the great elm tree fell, we found an abandoned kitten inside a hollow trunk by the garden wall. It was dark smoky grey with four white paws and very pointed ears, obviously hungry and completely wild. It took two days before we could catch it, and then it was only hunger and a longing for the saucer of warm milk placed invitingly by its lair which drove it out into the open. Wrapping up the snarling spitting little bundle in a thick towel I took it inside and tried to tame it. After a day or two it would eat a little and drink milk, but any attempt to go near to it produced a miniature fighting tiger, and a headlong flight up the velvet curtains. Our household cat considered it a definite outsider and the dogs would not come near it either, which was odd as usually they would adopt any young animal. After a few more days we left the door open and it fled, presumably to rejoin its wilder relatives. Domesticity was not its scene.

When we first moved from the Hall to the farm, we wanted a stable cat to keep down mice, and I went over to Auchtermuchty to pick up a kitten. When we got there, this small black cat was clinging to the top of a door, while two collies lay down below, and it was petrified. Again wrapping it up in thick towelling, I put it in my younger daughter's arms, and we set off on a noisy journey home, accompanied by a series of eldritch howls. By the time it was esconced in a warm stable with milk and cat food and my adoring daughter, it had been christened Coka Cola and become part of the family.

This did not satisfy its domestic instincts and a month later there were terrible howlings in the night, and a missing Cola, while my dogs were hurling themselves in fury first at one door and then at another. I let them out and they roared out into the darkness, and Cola shot inside, looking very bedraggled. Four weeks later and our half grown kitten cat was looking distinctly bulgy and as the nine weeks gestation passed, we prepared a padded cardboard box in a corner of the stable. Sure enough six beautiful kittens appeared, although my daughter was the only one allowed near. She reported that they were all beautiful, which went without saying as she is besotted by cats, and all had four white paws, and tabby striped bodies. As they grew larger, Cola decided that they were not safe in their cardboard box, and removed them one by one to the hay loft, carrying them dangling from her mouth by the scruff of their necks. All went well, until the kittens were ready to go to new homes. That night there were more caterwaulings in the night, and more infuriated dogs, and the following morning we found a distraught Cola, and six dead kittens. Their wild father had come back and killed the lot.

Deep woe prevailed, although the fastest to recover was Coka Cola, who soon started to look bulgy yet again. This time we provided a secure anti wild cat retreat and in due course six more beautiful kittens appeared. Like the others they were larger than normal, darkly striped, and most had four white feet. Their ears were more pointed than Cola's, and their tails longer with rows of rings going down from top to tip.

The wild cat never came near during the day when the dogs and people were around, and Cola spent her daylight hours rounding up her wayward brood. Once we heard her crying in distress, and ten feet above her head dangled one of the kittens. It was clinging for dear life with the tips of its tiny claws caught on the edge of the loft door, and its hind legs scrabbling for purchase on the old grey stones. We rescued it and returned it to Cola, who seized it by the scruff of its neck and set off with stiff wide steps back to her place of safety, its back legs trailing limply on the ground as she marched it off in disgrace.

We found good homes for all the kittens, and rushed Coka Cola to the vet to be neutered before any more litters appeared. Not only did we not want any more kittens, and cats can produce up to four litters a year, but Cola was looking very tired and bedraggled by her maternal efforts, and as she was a very small little black moggy in any case, further litters could have killed her. One of her kittens went down to the borders with the same groom who bought Danny, and the last I heard it had grown as large as a corgi and had killed a dog which tried to steal its supper. The wild cat must have fathered both litters.

Cola is still with us, now thirteen years old, and almost circular with age and good living, and endless titbits fed to her by a doting Granny. Occasionally she gets stuck in the cat flap, and is then put on a diet to reduce her well fed purry self to a more respectable size. She is a very different cat from the stable moggy who used to sleep on the back of the Shetland pony.

After we had been at the farm for three years, we acquired a second cat, as the result of an accident. My daughter was travelling by scooter, complete with flute, to play in a concert in St. Andrews, and as she was driving along a car overtook her, slowed down slightly and the passenger threw a young cat straight out of the window onto the verge, catching it with a wheel as it went. Horrified, my daughter slewed to a stop and cradled it in her arms. It was barely alive, and she rushed to the vet, with the cat tucked into the front of her jacket, but by the time she got there the animal was dead. She arrived home very distressed, and we decided that since we could not do anything for it, we would acquire another kitten instead.

This was how our second cat, called Scrap Heap,

came into our lives. One week after she arrived, my daughter left for college, and I inherited the cat. This time I played safe and Scrappie was swiftly neutered, and she has grown into a very handsome tabby with symmetrical markings, and a deft paw at catching mice.

All cats will chase moving things, and one day Scrappie was sitting on a gatepost in the sun by the manure heap, watching the world and the horses go by. There was a breeze blowing, and the horses were cantering round the field with their tails up, full of the joys of Spring. A pony called Conker trotted by a yard from Scrappie, with his white mane blowing in the wind, and with a bound, Scrappie had leapt onto the horses back, grabbing the maddening fluttering white hair with her claws. Conker broke into a startled canter, trying to get rid of his unwelcome rider, which made Scrappie dig her claws in still further. Conker started to gallop and the faster he went the harder Scrappie clung, until the two were careering round and round the field, like an act in a circus. Finally as they neared the gate for the third time, Scrappie let go and gave a wild leap for safety, landing in the soft stinking depths of the manure heap. Conker raced away to the end of the field, as far from equestrian cats as he could get, while Scrappie stalked off stiff legged with indignation to clean herself up.

My daughter now has two cats of her own, and has invested in a mechanical cat flap activated only by a gadget on the cat's collars, which is designed to exclude visiting admirers. This is a great game, as one of the cats, called Sable, has found that if she jumps back and forth a yard from the door, the flap will swing back and forth like a shuttle cock, giving little clicking noises. This adds a percussion aspect to this musical household.

Animals and birds will make use of what they find around them. Owls will take refuge in chimneys, and cats will ride ponies or play Tom Tiddlers ground with electronic gadgets if they get the chance. In many ways they are far more adaptable than human beings.

Chapter 8

"White Horses"

White horses are called greys, which is ridiculous, as a great deal of the time they end up white with brown streaks from rolling in the mud, or with green stripes from grass stains. Grey horses are also called grey with a qualifying word such as dapple or flea bitten, and to make it more complicated, many foals are born chestnut and some turn grey as they grow up, while some greys turn white for a few weeks each year when their spring coat comes in.

Shortly after we started up the riding stables we were offered the use of a grey pony some fourteen hands high, called Conker. He belonged to a girl who had gone away to college, and whose father had been sent abroad at the same time, leaving no-one able to care for a pony. When we went to collect him, we found him in a dark stable which had been flooded by recent heavy storms, and he was mired up to the shoulders, decidedly plump, and wild at being kept in without exercise. When first let out he was covered in black mud, and only the top of his head was white. All he wanted to do was gallop round and round the small paddock by the house, and it took us some time to capture him as he was desperately afraid of being put back inside. We saddled him up very carefully, padding the girth so that it would not rub his muddy stomach raw on the way to the farm, and putting a thick numnah under the saddle, to make it more comfortable.

Once there, in a clean airy stable thick with deep straw, we started to clean him up. Apart from the fact that his coat stank, we did not know whether he had cuts or sores beneath the encrusted dirt, so we had to be very gentle with him. It took a mixture of hot water, clipping, shampooing and hours of patient grooming before he began to look in any way presentable. Added to which he was completely unco-operative, and to begin with would not allow us to work on him for more than four minutes at a time. You had to have one person holding his head and stroking him into hypnotised somnolence while someone else tackled his muck ridden belly, and at frequent intervals he would wake up with a start, and throw his head up, or swing round and try to kick out. He was one very unhappy horse and very ticklish.

It took us three weeks to clean his coat up thoroughly, and another week or two for the clipped bits to grow evenly, by which time he was a different animal. Although he still disliked being groomed, he was friendly and pleased to see you, and he was a beautiful silky white with a luxurious mane and tail. Broad backed and sturdy, he was like a Connemara to look at, very comfortable to ride and generally well behaved, if kept apart from other horses. The problem was that as he had lived in an isolated spot, he was not used to other ponies or a lot of people and just didn't know how to behave "in company". Like a spoilt child he was either over boisterous or over friendly, and so once he was cleaned up we put him in a paddock on his own near the stables, so that he could become acclimatised to the big wide world.

He could see other horses on one side, and Granny's garden on the other, and spent his time bellowing his head off, and trotting up and down the perimeter fence with his head craning over it as far as it would go. After three days and nights, Conker had worn a muddy path all round his paddock, and was swaying on his feet from exhaustion, so we brought him in again for a rest, before putting him back in the field. The following morning he tried to jump out, and we found him lying flat on the ground looking dazed with his legs tangled up in the wire. He lay quite still while we cut him free with the heavy wire cutters, and then rolled over and launched himself into a gallop bowling me and the cutters over in the process. When he had calmed down we put one of the older geldings in with him, and Conker immediately fell in love. He followed the other horse everywhere, one length behind, his eyes glued to its tail, and bellowed in panic if separated from his companion for a moment. After this we put various horses in with him, and he fell in love with each in turn before making friends with Snoopy, the black pony nearest in size as himself.

Although they are basically herd animals, most horses pair up with a particular friend and they will greet one another with whinnies and tossing heads, rubbing each other's necks with their nostrils, and nibbling up and down with their teeth, as though giving each other a friendly massage. This can go on for ages, with each animal getting more and more intense, and is a sign of affection. If you know a horse well, it may do the same to you, and it is well to remember that what seems a gentle nibble to a horse can easily turn into a painful nip on a mere human.

Horses are also snobs, and for preference will associate with animals the same height as themselves, and certain high bred animals will totally ignore little rough ponies unless there is no other animal near, when they will make friends with a donkey, a sheep or even a goat. They do not like being on their own.

One winter season we had a very beautiful mare called Millie in the stables. She was a dark dapple grey and nearly eighteen hands, and as she was so tall, she was put in the largest stable, which just happened to be next door to Conker. Now as I have said Conker liked other horses, but was not sure of the difference between mares and geldings, and he definitely had ideas above his station. The poor chap fell passionately in love with this beautiful and dignified aristocrat.

The stable wall between them was high and painted white, with black boards rising above, and by stretching his neck up as far as it would go, Conker could rest his nose on the corner above the manger and peer with open mouth and goggling eyes at his beloved next door. It was like a scene out of some Victorian seaside postcard, when you have a vulgar little boy peeping through the corner of a bathing tent at a lady in a state of elegant undress.

"He gazed at his beloved."

Millie ignored him completely: it was not that she treated him with disdain, because her manners were perfect, but she had eyes only for the bigger horses, and anything below fifteen hands did not exist for her. Conker suffered: not only from unrequited love, but from a stiff neck, and we had to move him away to a separate part of the steading until his beautiful princess left.

He obviously had a thing about grey mares, as the next he fell for was a pretty little twelve two pony called Mini, who was a terrible flirt. In the Spring we put them out in the big front field together with some other ponies to feed on the new grass, and when we went to retrieve Mini, Conker charged in between us and her and with flashing teeth tried to drive us off. It took three grooms, three long whips and a bucket of feed before we could separate them and get Mini safely out of the field. Heaven knows what she said to him, as afterwards they took a violent dislike to each other, and we had to keep them well apart; if a group of ponies were going out on a ride, the two would always have to be put at opposite ends of the string.

Sometimes if the weather was wet, and we needed the horses in the morning, we would put a group of them into the indoor school for the night with their individual haybags, and soft sand to roll in. They loved being inside in shelter, while the weather raged outside, and used to settle down happily, either sleeping stretched out flat on the ground, or dozing upright on their feet, occasionally changing their weight from one leg to another without opening their eyes.

Every so often we would renew the sand in the school, and one load of seventeen tons was a brighter colour than usual. Once it was spread we put in Conker, who was wet from rain, and a few of the other ponies, and left them rolling happily over and over to get the itches out of their skins. Late that night I checked that all was peaceful and the numbers were correct, and it was not until the following morning that we realised that no white Conker was present. Instead we had an extra chestnut. He had rolled and rolled until the red from the fresh sand had literally died him a rich reddish brown all over his body, with the exception of his tail, which looked like streaky bacon.

Out came the warm water and the shampoo and scrubbing brushes. After one application we had a horse whose body was the colour of pink marsh mallow, with a flowing white mane and tail, and it took three shampoos and several days before Conker returned to his normal pristine white.

After this he calmed down and became very useful in the stables. He did not like jumping over jumps in a paddock, but if he was out on a hack, he would happily hop over a tree trunk or any obstacle in his way. That to him was common sense, but like Warren, he regarded show jumping as a waste of time. Also you had to be very careful when you fed him, and once you had given him his bucket of feed, you left the stable fast. All horses can be difficult over food: after all it is the way they are trained, and it is one of the main motivating factors in their lives. The most dangerous thing you can do is to go into a field of horses, carrying a bucket of feed, because you will be surrounded by large hungry mouths attached to large hairy feet, and if you are not trampled in the rush, you are likely to get caught up in the middle of a kicking match.

If several horses are being hayed in a paddock it is wisest to feed number one horse first, and it is easy to know which this is, as horses will rapidly form their own pecking order. Also it is vital to put out enough hay nets, or piles of hay if the ground is dry, far enough apart, so that each animal can eat in peace. Once I forgot to be careful and after giving Conker a bucket of feed, I turned my back on him to pick up a fallen net from the stable floor. In a flash he was behind me and took a large bite out of my left buttock. Filled with fury, I roared at him and chased him round the stable for five minutes to teach him manners before retiring to examine my wounds. A perfect set of double teeth marks were rapidly turning blue as I looked at them, and although I healed up very quickly, it was a very annoying place to be bitten, as I could not exactly exhibit my wounds in public. After that Conker and I treated each other with great respect and I had no more trouble.

Another trick of Conker's was going to sleep at awkward times. I have seen him on a long trek in the forest, strolling quietly along behind the other horses, with his eyes tight shut, and a gentle snore bubbling from his nostrils. I swear he was asleep. Certainly if bored by a bad rider in a lesson he would deliberately shut his eyes and switch off completely, and it would take a sharp tap with a stick, or a bellow in his ear to get him to co-operate.

One hot day in summer, one of our instructors, who was always beautifully turned out, and extremely elegant, went out to fetch Conker in for a lesson, and did not reappear. Worried that something was wrong, I went out to find her dancing up and down with rage in her gleaming white jodphurs in front of Conker's gently snoring nose. She shouted, she thumped him, she hauled on the bridle with all her strength. Conker leant backwards a trifle and continued his snooze. I came up, slapped him sharply on the neck and said sternly

"Come on, Conker, snap out of it," and he came to with a jerk of the head, and meandered off towards the stables, followed by my apoplectic instructor.

There was no vice in him; once he had settled down, he was one of the easier ponies to deal with, and on one occasion when a very large lady rider tried to climb into the saddle, and somehow landed up with a large bust on one side of the crupper and an equally large stomach the other, Conker behaved perfectly. He stood rigidly with an expression of long suffering on his hairy white face, while she toppled over in slow motion and landed up underneath his belly, and he looked down his nose and blew gently at her hair as she crawled out between his front legs. Then he curled his top lip right back in a sneer, probably because he didn't like the smell of her shampoo, and gave a very loud yawn.

We became very fond of Conker. After all he was the only horse that arrived black, cleaned up to be white, and for a short interval changed into a chestnut.

Chapter 9

"The Yellow Peril"

During the Summer months we used to take the horses down to Tentsmuir for treks in the forest, and to do this we needed transport. After much soul and pocket searching we bought a Leyland Terrier lorry, divided it with partitions to take six horses, and called it "The Yellow Peril".

Once we had bought it, we had to learn how to drive it. Luckily we did not need a Heavy Vehicles Licence, as it was just below the qualifying weight, but having driven nothing but cars, I found it petrifying. I was taken out one morning by a friend of ours, who among other things was a mechanical genius with diesel engines. He instructed me very slowly and patiently, with cheerful little remarks such as:–

'Keep well away from the grass verge, or you will get stuck in the soft ground,' and

'Keep in the middle of the track as the edge is crumbling and you could tip over,' and finally, most crushing of all when I thought that the steering wheel was coming apart in my trembling hands:–

'Don't worry lass, the wheel is meant to tip upwards like that. It's the way it works!'

After half an hour of instruction I was shaking like a jelly, and retired discomfited to the kitchen for a soothing cup of tea, having declared that no way was this my scene, and that I would only drive in the direst of emergencies. Everyone was delighted. My husband said he did not know what I was making a fuss about, as lorry driving was dead easy when you knew how, and my eldest daughter gave a shriek of delight and shot into the cab of the lorry for an extended lesson.

The next problem was persuading the engine to start. This lorry ran on diesel, was underpowered, and unless it was run every day did not like waking up first thing in the morning. Like the cats it preferred to stay asleep. We invested in spray cans of quick start, referred to books of instructions, and received a great deal of helpful advice. I also bought a couple of strong tow ropes, and kept them handy in the back of my green Vauxhall.

Now it was obvious that if the lorry was full of horses, my poor little car would not be able to shift it, and in any case tow starting the Yellow Peril was a risky business. The farm lay at the end of half a mile of curving rough track, edged by fences and hedges and ditches, and the track was narrow, frequently muddy, and with only two places where you could pass another vehicle. Therefore before you started you had to make sure not only that the tow rope was firmly attached to the right portions of each vehicle, but that there was no obstruction between the farm and the road.

After a while we learnt that it was wisest to park the lorry facing the track, as towing it backwards was impossible, and if it was left facing the other way, the only place my car would land up would be either in the manure heap or in the indoor school. At least if we were facing the right way, I had a chance of escaping before the lorry trundled into the back end of my car.

Once I had started my patient little Vauxhall, I would have to rev the engine like mad and then ease in the clutch and try to tug the lorry out of its morning somnolence. This usually took several attempts, as the first time my engine would be cold and so it would stall, and the second time my foot would slip on the clutch and the tow rope would snap. This meant tying reef knots to join the ends together again. The third attempt was usually successful, and the car would stagger slowly ahead with grinding noises coming from the rear end, while the yellow giant behind lurched forward rocking gently from side to side as it hit the potholes. When both vehicles were moving in tandem, I had to drive faster and faster until the driver of the lorry let in the clutch with a jerk. The Vauxhall would leap abruptly backwards, and if the reef knots held, and the Diesel engine behind fired, we would proceed with dignity to the end of the track where we could separate the two vehicles and turn round to come back to the farm and load up. As a wake you up exercise it certainly beat physical jerks.

The horses soon became used to travelling in the lorry, and grew most enthusiastic about trekking in the forest. They obviously thought that it was far more interesting than circling round and round in circles teaching people how to trot, and also they needed higher quality feed, such as delicious oats or barley, and food is the most important item in any horse's day.

First thing in the morning they would be given a special feed suitable for their size and the amount of work they were going to do that day. This would send a ripple of expectancy through the stables. Next they would be thoroughly groomed, their hooves and their tack rechecked, while at the same time the diesel engine of the Yellow Peril would be forced into reluctant life and warmed up until it ran smoothly. The back of the lorry would then be opened up and the heavy ramp with its non slip ridges scattered with dry straw. The six horses and ponies who were going trekking that day would be brought out in turn, led up into their narrow compartments and their headcollars fastened to the wall next to a full haynet, to be shared on the journey with their next door neighbour.

This sounds simple but it was very important to place the ponies in the right order. For instance the weight had to be evenly distributed and those animals which did not like each other had to be kept a safe distance apart, so that they could not bite their neighbour's necks en route. There is nothing more unnerving than driving a lorry full of horses up a steep hill, and hearing world war three breaking out behind you. You cannot stop immediately, as if you do you will jerk the horses, who could then panic and slip, or hurt themselves some other way, and of course you will be unable to restart on the slope with their heavy weight behind.

Therefore when this happened it would be necessary to unload all the horses, lead them up to the top of the hill and then rebox them before you could continue. This procedure took several pairs of hands and if one horse proved unco-operative quite a lot of time. Meanwhile your trekking party would be waiting patiently for you in the middle of the forest.

We became expert at boxing the horses after a while, and they used to trot up the ramp like little lambs, with expectant expressions and mouths open to grab at their waiting haynets. Conker invariably went in last, and he was worth watching as he would walk up the ramp without being led, turn neatly sideways with his head facing left, and wait for you to tie him up. He loved the forest and like the others was capable of trekking four to six hours a day, two or three days a week. Even at the height of the season every horse had at least one rest day a week, when they were turned out into the field to relax, and some of them used to get most indignant when they saw the lorry departing without them.

We had a narrow escape one day. My husband was on his own driving the Yellow Peril back from the forest, fully loaded up with six weary ponies, when there was a loud honking from a car travelling behind. Thinking that one of the back brake lights had failed, he stopped and got out to investigate. The car driver rushed up saying:

"Did you know one of your wheels was wobbling around?"

A quick investigation discovered a very loose wheel, which might well have come off on a bad section of road. Someone must have forgotten to tighten up the wheel nuts, which had worked loose from the vibration over the rough tracks of the

"They trotted up the ramp like lambs."

forest. It was a very grateful driver who jumped up and down on the spanner to make quite sure that all the nuts were well and truly safe and he was very grateful to that honking car owner.

We had been giving riding lessons for a while before we obtained the concession to take treks out in the forest, and as this was a new adventure, we had to advertise. Each week I used to ring up the local paper with my selected advertisement, and my first attempt was definitely surprising:

"Hullo! Is that the Courier?"

"That's right Madam, which section do you want to advertise under," came the reply.

"I'm not quite sure. Can I just read out the advert and you can decide?"

"Certainly, Madam, go ahead."

I looked down at the back of the envelope on which I had scribbled the feed list and possible advertisements and started off:–

"Come to the forest. Treks for sale, one or two hour sessions."

There was a horrified gasp from the other end of the line.

"You can't say that, you'll be had up."

Mystified, I looked down again at my envelope. What on earth was wrong with riding lessons? I tried again.

"I don't see why," I said, "We've often advertised Trekking before, but not in the forest."

There was a shriek of laughter down the phone:

"I thought you said 'Sex for sale', not treks!" spluttered the operator between gasps. "Perhaps we'd better start again!"

After a very giggly few minutes, we finally decided on a suitable insertion which could not be misinterpreted, and this duly appeared the following Thursday under the column headed "Horses".'

We ran the treks for two or three summers, and they were hard work, but great fun, and they attracted all sorts of people, from beginners to experienced riders, so that we used to grade the various routes into easy, middling and hard, and take out extra escorts as needed for safety. We made some good friends and had some beautiful days out, but we did discover certain unexpected hazards. One of these was predatory females. There is something about riding schools that raises the libido of some people, and sometimes my husband would find that the odd female rider was out for more than just a trek in the forest. On these occasions, as he saw their coloured talons advancing, he would excuse himself for a minute and dash to the nearest phone.

"S.O.S., and bring some coffee," would come over the line, and I would get into the green car and head eastwards towards the sea and the forest. Once there in the clearing I would get slowly out of the car, wave and call out in ringing tones:

"Hello, darling, I brought the coffee," and a definite air of disappointment would descend on certain faces.

Predatory males were no problem, as female grooms learn early how to deal with them, and a man who cannot ride is at a distinct disadvantage at a fast trot, especially when in pursuit of a girl who appears to have ridden from birth!

Chapter 10

"Forest Rides"

Tentsmuir Forest was roughly divided by a grid pattern of hard roads and woodland tracks, and there were many beautiful places to ride. The Forestry Commission provided us with maps and a licence to trek, provided we kept to certain designated areas, and did not break up their road surfaces with headlong gallops.

The forest is large and to begin with it was very easy to get lost, but the horses soon came to know the regular routes, which varied according to the trekker's capabilities and whether we were planning on being out for one or two hours at a time.

When you take a string of horses out on a trek, you need to have a lead horse and a tail horse (generally known as tail-end-Charlie), both ridden by capable riders, and you should have at least one escort for every nine people on the ride. Experienced riders usually brought their own hard hats with them, but although it was not legally compulsory to wear them while trekking in the country as opposed to riding on hard roads, we always suplied hats and insisted that everyone wore them. This meant that while the back of the Yellow Peril was packed with horses and hay, the front cab would be stuffed full of grooms, sandwiches, saddlery and a score of assorted black and blue hats, as it was impossible to know in advance the size of the hatless heads waiting for you each day.

Nowadays most people wear skull caps, which are far safer but also much more expensive than the old hard hats, which needed replacing regularly, not just for cosmetic reasons but because if they were bashed in any way you were supposed to throw them out and buy fresh. We used to keep one battered old hat as an object lesson: the peak had broken off, and under the velvet cover there was a split in the rigid inner shell which stretched from forehead to crown.

The man who had been wearing it when he fell, had escaped with a bad headache, and the hat had certainly saved him from a fractured skull or worse. However careful one is when riding, it can be a dangerous sport and it is silly to take unnecessary risks, especially by refusing to wear protective headgear. After all even Olympic riders only get issued with one cranium per lifetime.

We learned early on that most people have no idea of what being able to ride means. Time and again we would ask the trekkers whether they could ride, and they would say confidently that of course they could, only to find out that their only equestrian experience had been on a stationary donkey on Blackpool beach. It was not that they were lying: they just genuinely thought that riding was as simple as sitting on a rocking horse in an arcade. Now although it is possible to teach the majority of beginners to ride well enough for a slow trek, which consists mainly of walking and trotting, it takes considerable more expertise to canter and jump, which is what every child brought up on Western films immediately wants to do.

There was one small boy who as soon as he was in the saddle with his feet in the stirrups, gave a loud yell and kicked his horse as hard as he could. His obedient mount took off at full gallop and the two disappeared into the trees, with the lad holding on to the saddle with both hands, while his petrified mother was left shrieking her head off in the clearing. This merely unsettled all the other trekkers, who stood around looking agitated, while the waiting horses just looked on with bored expressions. My daughter shot off on Prince to retrieve the would be cowboy, who was brought back much subdued about ten minutes later, and made to ride attached to a lead rein for the rest of the morning.

As this kind of thing was liable to happen, for safety's sake we spent the first part of each trek finding out people's capabilities, and we used to reserve special fun treks for those who we knew could ride well. Some of the beginners came back time and again during the summer and learned to ride very capably during the season, and it was very satisfying when a novice turned into an expert and was promoted to the faster treks.

The woods were criss-crossed by little streams and deeper ditches, which were fun to jump, and which provided much needed water for the ponies to drink. As we became used to the forest the horses would know before their riders which way to go, and would turn right or left and veer round corners like homing pigeons without being directed. This was fine with riders of little experience, some of whom were quite happy just to sit on the saddle, in some cases hanging on to the pommel with both hands, and meander quietly through the greenwood, admiring the beauties of nature around them.

Horses are fairly tolerant creatures on the whole, and if they have a novice or a nervous person on their back will usually treat him gently and look after him, but with a more experienced rider in the saddle, the horses assume that the rider will remain in situ, and will speed up accordingly. Therefore the problem came when we took out people who could ride, because if you were trotting along a grassy path and imagining yourself to be fully in control of your mount's actions, it was a little disconcerting when your horse suddenly swung sharply round a corner, leapt the fallen tree which you did not know was there, and broke into a fast canter across an open field. This is why it was so important to know how well trekkers could ride before you took them out, as otherwise you would have indignant riders falling off in untidy heaps all over the forest.

To avoid taking the lorry down twice in a day, we hired a field on the edge of the forest where we could safely leave some of the horses overnight. It made a useful staging post between the farm and the clearing, where hopefully everyone met at the start of the day. The Forestry Commission put up smart wooden signs for us pointing towards our start up area, and unless these had mysteriously vanished into the moonlight during the night, most people arrived at the right place about the same time. If fewer trekkers appeared than had booked, as often happened, we would have to leave one or two of the horses behind in a small paddock by the clearing, and although two animals would settle down together happily enough, one left on its own was liable to break out and come looking for its friends.

Barona was the largest of the horses we had, being over sixteen hands and very gentle, but he did not like being on his own, and one day as the ride returned happily to base, we came across him standing stock still in the middle of a track, looming over the bonnet of a small red Mini which had come to a halt in front of him, while its two frightened occupants gazed up in horror at this large hairy nose resting trustfully on their nice clean windscreen.

We retrieved Barona and apologised to the two motorists, and just to be helpful suggested that when they were in the south they might like to visit the wild-life park at Longleat.

One of the lovely things about Tentsmuir was that to the east the pinewoods sloped down to the sea, and you could take fast rides along the beach, and listen to the seals barking on the sandbanks a hundred yards off shore. Seals are curious creatures and some of them would swim towards you and bob up and down in the surf watching what was going on. Sometimes after a storm the babies would get stranded and you would find them asleep in the shelter of a dune. They look very soft and trusting with their great liquid eyes, but they also have very sharp teeth, and we used to encourage them to flop and flounder their way back to the water before they became dehydrated or attacked by dogs.

I have always liked seals way back from when I was a child in Ireland, and was sometimes allowed to ride the milkman's black horse along the beach, where the seals used to come up to the rock pools in search of stranded fish. Once at dusk I was taken down by my Father for a walk, and a man was sitting on one of the black weed fringed rocks playing an old violin. The haunted notes echoed out over the darkling sea, and the seals came up in a circle at the edge of the waves to listen. When the music stopped, they drifted away silently one by one until the beach was empty, and the magic moment was gone.

Sometimes in hot weather in summer, we used to take the horses swimming in the sea to cool off, and afterwards they had to be walked through a freshwater stream to avoid their hooves becoming brittle from the salt. The sea water was was very good for any little cuts or bruises or tick bites that the horses might have picked up that day, and one way of strengthening a horses legs is to go paddling in the sea. However, be wary while you do so, as some horses no sooner feel the lovely coolth of the water round their fetlocks than they have an overweening desire to roll. It is very hard for an inexperienced rider to prevent half a ton of horse from wallowing in the waves if it wants to and we made sure that everyone was well warned in advance of the possibility of a sudden unexpected bath, which was no good for either rider or saddle.

To keep a horse's hooves in good condition you have to appply hoof oil regularly to avoid cracks in the hard horn, and the easiest way to do this is with a pastry brush pinched from the kitchen drawer. Hoof oil is glutinous, black and sticky and children love using it, preferably when dressed up in nice white jodphurs for a show.

In summer you need to oil hooves frequently to avoid them drying out, and in winter you also need to vaseline the sole of the hoof in icy weather, to prevent snow and ice forming into a hard frozen ball, which compresses under the animal's weight and becomes trapped beneath the shoe. If not being ridden in winter it is in fact better and cheaper to have your blacksmith remove all shoes from a horse. They can always be replaced if not too worn when you want to ride again, and the animal is much more comfortable in harsh climes unshod. These frozen lumps are difficult to remove without warm water, and if they are not shifted the poor animal is left slipping and sliding around on four balls of slithery ice.

We did not trek in winter and reverted to giving lessons at the farm either in the field or in the indoor school. We also took out rides from the stables all year round, and our lead horse was usually Prince. This was not just because he was faster than any other horse we had, but he was a natural leader, who hated being overtaken by any other animal, and he was very useful as he could outpace any of the others, and turn on a sixpence when rounding up reluctant ponies like Misty. In an emergency my eldest daughter used to ride him bare back with leg aids only which left both her hands free to hold the reins of would be escapers.

If you were out on a ride and tried to keep Prince at the rear, he would walk faster and faster until he broke into a trot, and as his legs extended the pace would quicken util you would find that as usual you were back in the lead, where he had wanted to be all along.

Once, before we went to the farm, Prince was out early one morning on a beach near St. Andrews, which as everyone knows is the hallowed home of golf. At that stage in his life, Prince was not used to waves, and he took fright and managed to dump my indignant daughter wetly at the edge of the sea. He then took off at a gallop with reins trailing and headed back for his stable which was some miles away. Unfortunately he took a short cut straight across one of the greens, saw someone ahead and ground to a startled halt, leaving four parallel furrows in the precious turf. He then swung round, turned tail and proceeded on his way home, before being caught by a local man, and replaced in the stable where he belonged. The strange thing was that the damaged green was mended in a most curious way. It needed the generous application of two good bottles of whisky, and lo and behold the turf recovered overnight and we heard no more about it.

We were very lucky to be able to ride so freely in the forest, as it was the nearest you could come to a cross country event without the dangers, and the horses loved it. It was a sad day when after three years we had to stop the treks, and sold the lorry to a

"A short cut over the greens."

"man who worked the tatties". I expect that somewhere in the borders the Yellow Peril is still trundling slowly along the highways and byways, and being tow started by some reluctant vehicle or other in the early hours of the morning.

Chapter 11

"Green Caterpillars"

During the summer, we used to run residential courses for children from the age of seven to thirteen, and they used to arrive with armfuls of sleeping bags and teddy bears at nine o'clock on Monday morning.

We always seemed to have more girls than boys, and the aim of the course was to provide a child with a pony of its own for the week, to teach it to ride as well as possible during that time, and to have as much fun as we could while doing so. We also had classes in the care of horses, how to clean tack, how to muck out properly and how to lay a decent straw bed for a weary horse.

When they first came, the children were shown where they would sleep, which was in two attic bedrooms at the top of the stairs which led straight up from the front door. We had four beds of various sizes and shapes in each room, the windows of which looked out towards the hills and over the big field at the front of the steading. The front door opened into a sunny porch and a small inner hall, with a door each side leading to the drawing room and to what was generally known as the rumpus room, where everyone congregated if they wanted to be sociable or to watch television.

Once settled in we had an introductory session in the kitchen, learnt one another's names and explained what we were going to do that day. Then came the moment the children had been waiting for: meeting the ponies.

Each child was allocated a pony or horse suited to their size and ability, which was to be theirs for the week, and as some of our visitors had never ridden atall, the first things they were shown were how to behave in stables, how to approach a horse in safety and how to groom their fiery steed.

As soon as we reached the stables, everyone was issued with a named canvas bag of grooming kit, for which he or she was responsible, and which for hygiene reasons was to be used only on their own particular pony. These kits contained a curry comb, two brushes, each with the pony's name on it, and a hoof pick, and each bag was about eighteen inches by six, coloured navy or green, and came to us by courtesy of the local banks.

All horses love being groomed and fussed over, and there is usually an instant rapport between young children and ponies. They were shown how to brush the ponies until their coats gleamed, how to comb the manes without pulling too hard, and if the child was strong enough, how to check the hooves for bits of stone or grit. This took at least an hour, and after the gleaming horses had been inspected, everyone was herded into the kitchen for elevenses. Riding is exhausting work, and the last thing any instructor wants is to have a child passing out from lack of food, because he or she has been too excited to eat anything that morning.

With the inner man replenished, the children were taught how to saddle up and how to put on a bridle. This is not always easy, as some horses deliberately throw their heads up, and shorter children can be left dangling in the air and hanging onto the head collars for dear life. At this stage we had a rota of six helpers, who went from stable to stable helping and demonstrating, and when all the horses were ready we taught the children how to lead them into the school for their first lesson.

Some children learn very quickly, while others are too nervous or excited to concentrate, but by the end of the second day most of them could trot a little, and by the end of the week, most could canter and ride well enough to have fun in the final gymkhana in which everyone took part.

We had a wide variety of children from all sorts of backgrounds on the courses, and some used to come back year after year, growing in size and expertise each time. They ranged from seven year old Jason, who had the longest eyelashes I have ever seen, to languid would be beauty queens of fourteen, who worried about the state of their nail varnish and felt sick at the sight of a dirty stable. One of the advantages of the farm was that it was two miles from the nearest village, so would be escapees in search of the bright lights had nowhere to go, and in any case by the end of a day of physical exercise most of them were pleasantly tired, and content to read or talk, or take part in the various knock out competitions which were run each week.

Most of them knew how to play a few simple card games, or Monopoly, but by the end of their holiday, they had learned how to play Draughts, Scrabble, Chinese Chequers and a game called Othello, which consisted of turning over black and white discs in order to capture your opponents counters, and which was the most popular game of of all. Of course everyone won a prize of some sort whether it was for becoming a board game champion or for having the best turned out pony. Every single child was good at something, and as they were always busy, they were happy, and so were we.

Every one had to have breakfast before they went out to the stables in the morning. "No breakfast, no riding" was the rule, regardless of how they ate when they were in their own homes, and they had to swallow at least one piece of toast before they were allowed to put one wellie booted foot outside the door. Sometimes we would take a picnic down to the beach and split the course into two: I would take the smaller children down for a bathe and a paddle, while the more advanced riders had a jumping lesson, or as a special treat were taken for a hack in the forest. Several of the children had never seen the sea in their lives, and at their first sight of the great expanse of waves breaking on the sand, they would stand absolutely still, while their eyes would grow as big as saucers. I remember Jason and another small boy slithering on their tummies through the shifting sand pretending to be seals, and you could practically see their flippers and feel the cool wetness of the imaginary waves on their smooth brown backs.

We had several children from the tower blocks in Glasgow, and they were enormous fun to teach.

Their first reaction when they arrived was to run round and round jumping up and down in sheer delight at being in a wide open space where they could make a noise. In the evening some of them would go out to the indoor school and play tag, or just race about under the arc lights pretending to be horses and cowboys and trains and steam engines. Children have marvellous imaginations and the best time of all was when they dressed up themselves and their mounts for the fancy dress competition. This was part of the final gymkhana in which local children also competed, and was inspected by outside judges, so there was great excitement beforehand. They could use anything they could con out of me to dress up in, other than their sheets and pillow cases, and the carpets off the floor, and we had everything from Dick Turpin on a black masked Bess, to Ena Sharples in her curlers and old bedroom slippers.

In one of the best competitions held at the end of May, long suffering Barona was dressed up with straw tied round his legs and his rider disguised as Wurzel Gummidge the scarecrow. A plump little white pony called Pansy was arrayed in black suspenders, stockings and lacy bra round her chest, while her equally plump little rider posed blue and shivering in a bikini on her lace edged saddle. Pretty little Mini the grey pony was arrayed with garlands and her rider as Queen of the May, while one of the older boys came as a railway engine, complete with cardboard cow catcher attached to the horse's martingale. Once we had the lazy lion from the "Wizard of Oz", a Cybernaut and a black winged vampire straight from Transylvania, followed by Conker as Pegasus, and last but not least a sleepy Snoopy ridden by the Archangel Gabriel.

We took every possible precaution to keep the children safe, but it was not possible to foresee every danger, and one hot afternoon there was very nearly a nasty accident. After lunch each day the children had a quiet half hour in their rooms before going riding, and we had provided them with coloured pens and a hard backed book which was to be their diary of the course, with prizes for the most beautiful creation.

All was peaceful when there was an almighty bump on the top landing, followed by a series of muffled thumps, which grew louder and louder, until there was a final slithery noise and an ominous crash at the foot of the stairs.

I rushed to the front hall to be faced by a seething mound of green sleeping bags, and a tangle of arms and legs and heads. Pulling them apart I separated out seven hot little bodies, and sat them down in the front porch to find that underneath the lot lay the smallest and youngest girl of them all. She looked very squashed and decidedly dazed, and it took me several minutes to peal off the nylon sleeping bag which had grown sticky from the heat, and seemed to cling to her flushed skin like glue. Once she had recovered the breath which had been squashed out of her by the combined weight of the other six children, she seemed perfectly alright, and I sat down and asked what on earth they had been playing at.

"Nothing much," came the answer, "we'd

"I'm sure there were seven at lunch!"

finished our diaries so we thought we'd all dress up as green caterpillars and see who could wriggle to the bottom of the stairs first!"

After this we added another safety rule: to our list:- "Thou shalt not dress up as a green caterpillar and jump down the stairs after lunch."

All of which only goes to prove that you cannot foresee everything.

There was one pair of teenage girls who arrived together and whenever we suggested that they groom a horse, learn to trot, or much out a stable only said in chorus:–

"I canna dae it."

This was most discouraging and after twenty four hours I forbade them both to say it ever again, pointing out that how did they know that they could not do something unless they had had a go. After that they started to say:–

"I canna dae it, but I'll try."

This was at least a slight improvement, and by the end of the week both had learned to trot and canter and even to take a horse over some small jumps, which was a great achievement, and I was very proud of them. By the time they left, they promised me that when something was suggested like learning a new sport, they would at least say:–

"I'll try," and I am sure that they will do just that.

Time passes swiftly when you are happy, and by the time Friday came we all felt that we had grown to know each other very well. Parents would collect their children any time after four oclock, and some would arrive earlier in order to see their children riding and taking part in the final gymkhana events, and prize giving.

Some children would stay for two weeks at a time, and were regarded with envy by those who had to leave us. Sometimes a child could not be found, and would be finally winkled out from the middle of the hay loft or some other place where they had hidden. We had to point out that it was not very kind to greet your ever loving parents with tears and demands for another week at the farm, and to ease the pain of parting with their beloved week's pony, we took lots of photographs and sent them on the way with prizes for whatever they had been best at, with special awards for those who had tried the hardest.

I loved running the courses. Some of the busiest and happiest times in my life have been passed among children and ponies, and I am sure that in an ideal world every child would have a dog to confide in and a pony to ride.

Chapter 12

"A Different Drum"

Small children and ponies have a natural affinity with each other, and in the same way those special children, the ones whose brains will never grow up, can identify with a horse and have just as much fun as any other child.

Animals always know instinctively if someone is handicapped, and in the same way that a sighted dog will run alongside and support one which is blind, so most horses will take special care of a subnormal rider.

The indoor school was ideal for this, as there was no chance of an animal running out, and we were protected from outside dangers such as weather or traffic. A group of adult riders used to come out occasionally from a hospital by minibus, and once there was a woman among them who was catatonic. She never spoke, but sat on a chair with her arms locked rigidly across her narrow chest, and her eyes staring at nothing. It took three people to lift her into the saddle, and to place her legs in the stirrups. Her tightly locked fingers were then gently un-curled and wrapped round the reins, and we started to walk, with one person leading the horse, and two more alongside in case she slipped.

At first it seemed as if she were not even aware of

being on a horse, and we walked quietly round the school talking all the time about the horse and the reins and what she should be doing if she were learning to ride. After five minutes, it was someone else's turn, and I unclasped her fingers from the reins and said,

"Time to get down now."

Very slowly she took her hands out of mine, and wrapped them round the reins again, and then she actually smiled. The nurses who had come with her were thrilled as apparently she had neither smiled nor reacted to what was happening around her for a very long time.

Another time Conker was walking around with a little girl on his back, who had very little strength in her legs, and as the child started to slip sideways, he stepped towards that side and with a neat little hitching movement of his shoulder, shook her back safely into the saddle, and continued round the school, as carefully as if he were carrying eggs in a basket. Mini also was a great help with beginners, and one day when an eight year old girl was learning to jump, the child slid down the pony's neck and landed unexpectedly behind her ears. Now the normal reaction of a horse if ridden like an elephant would be to drop its head and jettison its hapless rider. Mini didn't: she raised her head rigidly in the air, slowed her pace to a walk, still holding her rider aloft, and shook her gently back into the waiting saddle.

Sometimes we used to lunge blind riders. The instructor would stand in the centre of a circle with a long rope or lunge rein attached to the horse's bridle, and horse and rider used to walk, trot or canter round the perimeter of the school. This is the safest way to teach beginners, and it is a useful way of exercising a horse in bad weather.

Two of our horses, Prince and Misty, had been lunged and schooled so often, that if we wanted to exercise them in winter, we used to take them into the school without saddle or bridle, and put up two small jumps at opposite sides of the building. We would then call out:–

"Walk on, and t-rot,"
and they would both start trotting one behind each other. Once their muscles were warmed up the next command would come:–

"And canter,"
and they would break into a canter and circle round hopping over the jumps in turn. After five minutes or so, the next command would be:

"And turn,"
and they would wheel round in unison and start off in the opposite direction.

In the same way these two, Prince and our schoolmaster Misty knew what to do in lessons without even being told, and if there were a child riding in a gymkhana who was not very able, we would mount them on Misty or Badger, and they would inevitably win. You only had to point Badger towards a set of bending poles, and he would dash ahead bouncing neatly in and out like an animated brown rubber ball, regardless of what his inexpert rider thought that they were telling him to do. All they needed to do was to sit there and hang on very tightly, and they would win the race.

We had painted the letters A to H round the walls of the school, to assist with dressage lessons, and if we had small children learning to ride, it was fun to have simple competitions like

"Find a big A", or "Touch a big C".

In this way, if a lesson was made into a game which everyone could understand, then it was a success, because young children easily become bored and lose concentration, but even the youngest in mind usually knew the first few letters of the alphabet.

When we took blind or partially sighted riders outside, they would be led by someone walking alongside, or held on a leading rein from another horse. Occasionally if there were only one or two we would take them out for a quiet hack in a line of other horses all following after one another.

We also had one blind man who came to ride, who was one of the best riders I have ever seen. He was not satisfied with the quiet little hacks: he wished to jump, and jump he did in the indoor school, with the instructor counting out the paces between each jump, until he grew used to the distances involved and managed on his own. How he had the courage I never knew. It takes a lot of guts to launch oneself over four foot fences even when you can see them, and he was jumping blind and trusting his horse to carry him through. Maybe sometime it will be possible to transplant eyes, so that the blind may see again. That would be a miracle worth having.

Many children came to the stables, and there was one whom we will call Billy. He was described by his mother as backward, but he was quite capable of learning provided you took him slowly through the lesson, and demonstrated what you wanted him to do. He was not so good on understanding verbal instructions, as his vocabulary was limted, but he soon managed to trot and canter tolerably well. The trouble came when he was told to lead his pony Badger out to the field and to take off the headcollar before turning him loose. Now Badger was very gentle with Billy, but each of them was as obstinate as the other, and when Billy did not reappear, I went out to see what was holding him up.

From the gate I could see Billy and Badger standing face to face, about three feet apart, and both were absolutely still. I couldn't make out what was happening, and then I realised that Billy had tried to remove the headcollar without undoing the buckle, and had simply grabbed hold of it and pulled. Badger had immediately tugged in the opposite direction and there they were stuck like statues, with Billy's arms rigidly outstretched, and Badger's legs locked forward in protest at this uncivilised treatment.

After disentangling them and putting Badger out for a well earned mouthful of grass, I returned with Billy back to his mother.

"Billy," I said, "when you take your trousers off at night, don't you undo the braces first?"

"No, I don't," replied Billy, looking up at me with trusting brown eyes.

"That he doesn't," broke in his mother, looking down at him proudly, "Nor with his shirt neither; he just pulls it over his head and all the buttons come off. Like shelling peas it is, and I'm for ever sewing the dratted things back on again!"

There was another child called Ian, who while not handicapped either physically or mentally certainly had a great deal to contend with in his young life. He lived on a small holding some distance away, and his father was so determined that his small son should learn to ride, that he booked a course of private lessons with one of our instructors. In fact so determined was he that when young Ian did not do exactly what the instructor said, his proud papa leapt into the ring and threatened to belt him one.

Now riding lessons are meant to be enjoyable, and after removing Ian's father to the kitchen for a soothing cup of coffee we had a good look at this oddly shaped six year old. He was dressed in slightly baggy brown cord trousers, black boots and a padded brown anorak, and he looked like a miniature Michelin man. His arms and ears stuck out each side almost at right angles and his face was scarlet from heat and embarrassment. Obviously there was no way his muscles were going to be able to work properly when he was wrapped up like an Egyptian mummy, and so we started to remove the brown top layer. Underneath we found another padded anorak, three thick jerseys, and finally underneath that a heavy cotton long sleeved shirt.

"My Mum thought I might be cold," said Ian unnecessarily, and added that he felt better now.

After his cheeks had returned to a normal healthy pink we proceeded with the lesson, and when it was over wrapped him up again and sent him on his way, with instructions to wear fewer layers the following week.

His riding gradually improved, until one day he arrived unable to keep his eyes open. Worried that he was sick we asked what the matter was, and he said he hadn't been able to sleep for the last few days because of the pigs.

"How on earth can the pigs keep you awake?" we asked.

"It's all the piglets," said Ian, "Dad said it was too cold for them outside and put them all in with me. Eight of them there are. they won't keep still and they squeals all the time."

I had a vivid mental vision of Ian tucked into bed with four piglets on each arm, and agreed with him that it must make it very difficult to sleep.

"They wriggle about so," said Ian sadly, "and it keeps me awake."

There wasn't much point in teaching him that day so we cancelled the lesson and fed him on biscuits and milk in the kitchen while I read the paper. Ian watched me quietly and then said:–

"What do you think of the Arab question?"
I looked at him in astonishment, and he pointed to an article on Libya at the bottom of the page. It was a very adult question from such a small boy.

"What do you think of them?" I replied curiously.

Ian put his elbows on the table, wiped off a milky moustache with the back of his hand, and proceeded to hold forth at length on the problems of

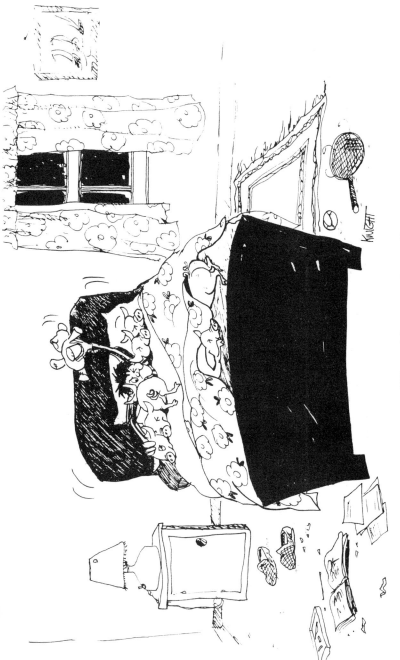

"Four piglets on each arm."

the Middle East. Out rolled long words and learned opinions more suited to a sixty year old professor than a sleepy six year old boy.

"Where did you learn all that?" I asked, and he answered nonchalantly.

"My Dad and I talk, and anyway I'm seven next week."

Ian eventually learned to ride, and his instructor was endlessly patient with him as he was not really interested in horses. He was however determined to please his Dad, who was spending all this money on his lessons, and I am sure that whether he ends up as a farmer or a professor or something more adventurous, Ian will go far.

Not all fathers bother to talk to their sons, and we had another small boy called Jack, who was unteachable. He just made no effort at all and we could see no physical or mental reason why we were not getting through. Finally I sat him down and asked him why he was not trying.

"I don't want to learn to ride," replied Jack simply.

"Then why come here at all?" I asked.
Jack looked at me, wriggled his shoulders and rubbed the front of one boot against the back of the other.

"You won't be cross will you," he said looking down at the sandy floor of the school.

"No," I replied, "I won't be cross but I would like to know."

Jack heaved a deep sigh and the corners of his mouth turned down.

"You see," he said, "I was given a racing bike for

Christmas, but I'm not allowed to touch it until I can ride a horse."

Most children are lovable, and the mongols most of all. There was one boy called David, who was heaven to teach. In the same way as we taught the blind riders, we started off with David being led and with a strong armed catcher walking on either side. He would sit quietly for a minute and then look up at us and laugh for cheer joy in being alive. Sometimes he would make an attempt at a trot, bouncing up and down energetically in the saddle, and then without warning would launch himself into space like a rocket. David learnt a little and enjoyed everything, and we always felt good after he had been with us. Like so many of these special children of God, he had the gift of sharing happiness. There was nothing wrong with him, he just danced to a different drum.

Chapter 13

"The Reactor"

Black Dancer was jet black, fourteen two hands high, and jumped anything he was asked to. I bought him from a girl who could no longer keep him, and he came to us at the same time as Snoopy, Barona and Brutus.

When we first saw him we were warned by the nervous looking owner that he could be dangerous, as he sometimes reared up and tried to throw his rider. Now this kind of animal is no good for a riding stables, but at first sight he certainly did not appear threatening in any way. He stood there quietly looking out over the top of the stable door, with a wisp of hay hanging from the corner of his mouth.

His owner brought him out of the stable saddled up and with a pelham bit on. This looked ominous as this particular bit of hardware is used for runaway horses, and is extremely harsh on an animal's mouth. Then she clanked her way to his near side and I saw that she was wearing spurs.

No sooner was she in the saddle than she dug in her spiked heels and yanked hard on the reins. With pain from the spurs goading him on and the pelham biting into his mouth inevitably the poor horse reared up. She rode him around for a short while and then I asked if we could try him out.

After talking to him for a moment or two, my groom mounted up and squeezed Black Dancer's sides gently with her legs. Nothing happened. She kicked gently with her heels and he moved smoothly forward, and eased into a slow trot. She cantered round slowly, hopped over a couple of low jumps, and as long as she did not pull hard on his mouth, he behaved like a model horse. In fact he seemed ideal for the stables and so we bought him and took him back to the steading.

When he arrived he had a long mane, and although his coat shone, he kept scratching his neck and tail up against the stable door. On close examination we found that not only did he have a sore mouth, but he was suffering from sweet itch, which is a kind of allergy rash at its worst in hot weather, and which we treated with oil and powders and by hogging his mane to keep him cool.

Without his long black mane his coat shone sleekly, and when ridden in a simple snaffle his mouth soon healed and there was no need for anything stronger. Far from being dangerous, he was in fact rather sluggish, and like Snoopy liked being idle. However he was very gentle natured, and got on well with the other horses right from the from the beginning. Personally I found him a delight to ride, as he was completely reliable and very comfortable. Unfortunately for me everyone else had the same idea, and he became a general favourite.

He did however have one small trick, which we discovered the first time we took him out. A quarter of a mile down the farm track a little bridge crossed over a stream, which pretended to be a river in times of heavy rainfall. When rides started out they had to cross over this structure, which was a mixture of concrete slabs and railway sleepers, and which caused me to quiver with trepidation whenever a heavy lorry came to the farm. The ride started out peacefully enough, until this half way point was reached.

Black Dancer then stopped dead, dug in his heels, and flatly refused to cross the running water with a rider on his back. Patiently we led him to and fro over the small bridge, until he grew used to it, but he turned out to be equally nervous about puddles, and we found that he would either sidestep round them, or hop over the top. There was no malice in him, like Canute he just did not like getting his feet wet.

The next problem we had with him came in late summer, when I went into the stables early one morning and found that Black Dancer had swollen cheeks and looked like a koala bear. Roaring with laughter I rang the vet and said that we had a horse which appeared to have mumps, and was it serious. Out rushed our friendly vet muttering horrid words like "strangles" under his breath, and filling me with foreboding. By the time he had finished examining the horse, the swelling was visibly shrinking, and Black Dancer looked supremely unworried. I put him out in he front field, and he wandered happily down to the stream for a drink. Reluctant as ever to get his feet wet, he stood there on the bank, his black coat gleaming against the creamy yellow blossom of the wild meadow sweet that grew along the water's edge. Specks of pollen floated through the air and he dropped his nose gently into the cool water.

A quarter of an hour later his cheeks were again extended like monkey pouches. As I sneezed my way back across the field we realised that he was allergic to that particular plant. Black Dancer suffered from hay fever, which is a most inconvenient ailment for a horse.

After this episode we christened him "The Reactor", and in Summer kept him inside away from the meadow sweet, and we also dumped his haynets in a bucket of water before hanging them up to drip. This had the effect of damping down the pollen, but did not affect the hay in any other way, and Black Dancer nibbled cheerfully away, without any more sneezes and wheezes. We also kept a wary eye on him for any more bulbous or itchy symptoms that might erupt, as he always seemed to be the first to suffer.

The next time he had a reaction, we all suffered. A nearby farmer had given us warning that he was going to spray his fields, and duly on the day we kept in the horses, and watched from afar this helicopter flying back and forth, trailing clouds of chemicals over the green fields on the far side of the valley.

Twenty four hours later, our Reactor, Black Dancer was streaming from the nostrils and had all the symptoms of a very bad cold, including runny eyes. Added to this we were all coughing: every horse, every groom and all the family were going about hawking and spitting, and the only ones unaffected were the cats and dogs.

Farm sprays can produce all sorts of reactions, and a cold or cough, or a skin complaint can spread through stables like wildfire. Therefore, if you have many horses it is important that each should have its own grooming kit to prevent cross infection, in the same way that it is unwise to use a comb belonging to someone else on your own hair. Also it is important that anyone regularly handling horses and the resulting manure should be up to date with their tetanus injections, and nowadays children should have these automatically along with their measles and hooping cough immunisations.

Stable hygiene is important and each year as soon as the warmer weather came and we could put the ponies out in the fields, we used to spring clean the stable block. This meant cleaning out all deep litter or straw from the stalls, which was back breaking work, and then scrubbing down walls and doors with a diluted disinfectant like Jeyes fluid. Once dry the walls were white washed and all woodwork treated with creosote, which was great fun to do, and reduced the insect population and any nasty little bugs temporarily down to zero.

One day during this annual clean up I mislaid all three grooms and was standing in the middle of the half painted stables yelling my head off, when from behind the low white wall of one of the stalls appeared what looked like a comedy trio of goons. Three battered woolly caps, spattered with white, topped three sets of streaky blue overalls, and three leprous looking right hands held aloft three large dripping brushes. The working party was enjoying itself!

"The working party."

When finished the steading looked beautiful and fresh, with the exception of the harness room wall, where some bright eyed enthusiast had painted whitewash on top of creosote, which had interacted with each other producing a bubbly blotchy mess.

Someone else had also painted the downstairs loo shamrock green, and best of all the white sliding doors of the indoor school had a vivid black cartoon of horses and ponies whose riders seemed to be either flying through the air, or else landing in uncomfortable positions on the hard hard ground below.

The most serious infection we had in the stables, was when a visiting horse erupted with ringworm, possibly carried on its saddle, and we had to screen every horse in the place, and isolate the victim with barrier nursing. By this time there were twenty two horses altogether, and this involved taking them in relays into the indoor school after dark, and shining an infra red light on their coats.

It was an eerie scene, with the half visible shapes of the animals moving about under the queer violet light, and we picked out two who had a few marks on their coats which glowed phosphorescent in the dark. Both had been treated earlier that year with an antiseptic cream which produced the same luminous sheen under infra red, and we could see no sign of any skin infections on them. However to be on the safe side, I bought a large tin of white powder and dosed everyone and every animal in turn, right down to the poor old dogs and cats, who strongly objected to the taste. This was one occasion when our Reactor did not react, and his coat remained its normal shiny black.

Reactions in people and animals can be extremely odd, and once when we had children staying for the week, I took them out into one of the fields to show them how dowsing worked. Water Companies use a special meter, or copper rods, which do the same thing as the traditional hazel twigs, from which I could never get any reaction atall. I supplied each child with a couple of metal coathangers, and cut these with wire cutters into an L shape, with a long upward arm, and a short base.

I then lined them up holding the short sides of their rods in each inward facing fist, with their thumbs lying on top of the longer side, and we all walked forward over the field which was full of land drains, which lay underground every twenty yards.

It is a funny feeling when the rods start to twitch, and the children were fascinated. I tried this several times, and well over half could dowse a little, though the reaction varied in strength. When the rods cross over each other, there is water below, and if they swivel to one side they are pointing to the source of the flow.

Obviously none of us were expert, and we had no idea how deep down the water was, but it was fun to do. Albert Einstein thought that dowsing worked by electromagnetism, and that in the same way that migrating birds navigate by responding to the earth's magnetic field, so the dowswer's muscles reacted unconsciously to minute fluctuations caused by water or minerals below ground. Whatever the reason, it works, and I used to find it very useful if we had a leak in our water supply, which was piped from the nearby farm, or as a

Chapter 14

"Dangerous Practices"

It is easy to look on ponies as cuddly little toys, but they are not. They are large hairy mammals, which need strict discipline and careful treatment if you are going to live with them safely. A horse behaves well because it wants to please you, and has been taught that if it doesn't something unpleasant will happen. After a horse is broken it knows what to do, but trust between you can only build up gradually, when you are respected as leader of the herd, or "One who must be obeyed".

It is hard to believe that animals of such beauty can harm you, and often the best looking horses are full of the nastiest tricks. We had one such mare, a bright chestnut in colour and very showy, called Cora, who looked as if butter would not melt in her mouth. She would behave like a golden angel when being tacked up, and with other horses her behaviour was impeccable, but if she could crush your leg against a gatepost or trap your head against the wall in a stable she would, and we treated her with extreme caution for the short time she was with us. She was unusual in that she did not seems to like people, and if a horse is not naturally friendly then it is not worth having, as you will always have to be on your guard.

It is illegal to use a horse under five years old for lessons in a school, as young animals are unpredictable. If they are startled by a passing plane or an exploding pheasant they may run out or throw their rider, as their first instinct when frightened is to run away, and of course they can run much faster without a weight on their backs. Beginners especially are much safer on older schoolmaster ponies such as Misty, because they are less excitable and not so easily scared, and even then it pays to be careful.

Certain riders suit certain horses, and it is no good putting a young man on a skittish mare, which behaves better with a woman on her back, or small girl on a horse so wide backed that she bounces about like a pea on a drum.

One time to be cautious is when you let a horse loose in the field after a ride. Never lead it to the gate, thump it on the rump and yell
"Away with you"
in hearty tones, as it is liable to kick out in ecstasy at being free, or charge past you at thirty miles an hour. I did this once years ago, and the swish of the horse's heels as he bucked and lashed out missed scrambling my brains by a bare quarter of an inch! The right way is to lead the horse into the field, turn its head back towards the gate and then quietly take off the headcollar. This way you have time to walk away and the pony has to turn round before heading for freedom.

Another nasty trick is rolling plus rider. Brutus was a horse that adored rolling, and as soon as his saddle was taken off, it was wise to stand well back, as he would bend at the knees and sink blissfully onto the ground, into the sand, or wherever he happened to be. Over and over he would roll, rocking back and forth, with his tummy in the air, legs waving like broken lamp posts above him, and eyes closed in bliss. This would continue until all the nasty itchy places had gone from his back, and he would get up and shake himself vigorously, before trotting off for a drink and a mouthful of grass.

No-one minded Brutus rolling when untacked, but he also adored the feel of water, and if you were riding across a shallow river, or on the edge of the sea, Brutus would stand still and his eyes would start to close. This would be a warning signal that the knees were about to bend, and there would be a concerted shout to the unwary rider of

"Quick! Pull him up hard, and keep his head high,"
as otherwise Brutus would go down in slow motion, saddle and all, tipping his rider off as he went, and the end result would be a soaked saddle and a sodden horse. It didn't do the riders much good either.

Most accidents happen when one is in a hurry. A horse will know its own particular stable and will usually go straight to it, but you can be sure that if you let two animals loose at once, they will both make for the same stall, or collide in the doorway, with you as punchbag in the middle. Other dangerous moments are putting on a saddle, as some horses are very ticklish just behind their forelegs, and will deliberately turn and nip as you tighten up the girth. Grooming stomachs can be a dicey operation for the same reason, and it is sensible to fasten the headcollar to the wall ring before you start, and

"A soaked saddle and a sodden horse."

to stand well back to avoid a sideways kick. Well behaved horses do not do these things, but wicked little ponies often do, and it is best to keep a wary eye open until you know your animal very well indeed. Like children horses will often play up just to see how much they can get away with.

Feed time can also be a danger area. In the wild animals compete for food, with the strongest eating first and best. It is wise to leave a horse to eat its food in peace, and to make sure that piles of hay in a field are far enough apart, so that the horses can play musical chairs without kicking each other, and even the lowest in the pecking order does not go hungry.

We had one nasty accident with Prince in Yorkshire, just after he was broken. Right from the first time they rode, it was an absolute law that both my daughters should always wear a hard hat, even if just riding through the yard, and this saved my eldest daughter's life. She had been out for a ride, with me walking alongside, and after Prince was untacked, she prepared his hot feed, and hat on head and bucket in hand leapt up on to his bare back to take him through to his stable.

I was about twenty yards away and I could see what was going to happen, but could do nothing to stop it. The hot side of the feed bucket touched Prince's ribs and burnt him, and he reared straight up and lunged forward at full gallop. My daughter was thrown up into the air, still holding the bucket, and from then on everything seemed to happen in slow motion.

The hot feed cascaded down towards the ground

and she turned half a somersault and landed with a sickening crunch on the stone flags of the yard, with her head banging against the step of the stable.

She was lucky: the hat took the force of the fall. Its peak snapped in half, and on the right side there was a dent half the size of a tennis ball. She was left with a king sized headache, and a mass of bruises, but if she had not been wearing that hard hat, I doubt if she would be alive today.

Next come the dangers that you cannot guard against. In many ways you are safer out on a hack, than in a jumping ring, but all roads have their hazards. One afternoon we were taking out a ride down towards a small harbour, which lay at the base of a long hill. There was never much traffic, and the ride used to proceed in single file down the narrow lanes. All the horses were walking quietly, when a bright yellow car, full of youths roared past, and as they went one of them threw a squib at Brutus' feet. Naturally he was startled, but he was good as gold, and just stood like a rock, until the ponies behind him calmed down, and the ride continued.

Another time a motor bike boy caught up with one of the grooms on Danny, the black pony, and circled round and round trying to scare them, before stopping in a gateway to jeer. Now although Danny was only pony size, he thought of himself as a war horse, and prepared to protect his rider. He bared his teeth, gave a half rear and charged straight for the black leathered cyclist, who cowered back against the gate. The groom was a very good horsewoman, and she slid off Danny, grabbed his reins and hauled him down before he could pick up the youth in his teeth. She stood there with the furious horse holding the lad at bay, while she gave him a piece of her mind. Eventually she drew back and the motorcyclist climbed onto his bike and fled, and perhaps next time he might have thought twice before trying to cause trouble.

Some horses take exception to strangers in their fields, and geldings will protect mares, and mares their foals. Prince was very protective towards Bonny, the pretty little black mare we had when we first moved up to Scotland, and when two strange lads climbed over the fence and approached her, he put his head down and drove them straight out of the field, snapping at their heels as they went, and neighing with triumph as they vanished up the drive.

Another hazard was parents. One young couple used to come for lessons, and would park their five year Donald on the edge of the schooling ring, while they rode. We always kept a wary eye on children for their own safety, but this small boy was a menace. In the middle of the lesson, as all the horses were obediently trotting round, he drew a gun from his pocket and let off a series of caps. Two of the ponies shied, and a little girl was nearly thrown, before he was picked up and removed bodily from the field, followed by his anxious parents.

"Why on earth did you let him have a cap gun?" I asked.

"Well," said his Mother, "It's a new toy, and he wanted to bring it, and then he cried when we tried to take it away, poor little mite."

"He's so difficult to control you know, so we let him have it and thought it would be alright," added his Father apologetically. "After all nobody got hurt."

Needless to say, they were not welcome at the farm after this, and hopefully they removed the gun from dear little Donald before riding anywhere else. They did not come again.

There are always some people who regard riding stables as a dumping ground for kids, and you would find that one child would be dropped off for a ride, while three little brothers and sisters would be turned loose to play, usually without their parents even bothering to tell you. This was not safe, as the children could easily get hurt, fall in the stream, or wander off, and I had to keep a wary eye open to make sure this did not happen. Inevitably we always had lots of children around, and I loved having them, but they were there by invitation, and we knew when they arrived and what they were doing, so that everybody was happy. The farm was roomy and we often had young friends sleeping there for the night, either if they were going to help in the stables, or if they had an early ride or show planned for the following day and lived a distance away. They could then get up early and start plaiting and grooming at first light.

Stables are cheerful places, and never boring, as you always have to be prepared for the unexpected, whether it be run away tractors, ponies in the potatoes, or burst water pipes, but one time I was really caught out was on a peaceful afternoon in May.

Most of the ponies and horses were tied up in the yard being groomed, and some were being prepared for a nearby show the next day, when there was a clattering and a rattle, and round the corner of the track came a pony and trap. With the exception of Barona, who had seen it all before, every horse started wheeling round and rolling their eyes, and we had to shift the trap into the empty yard next door before we could calm all the animals down.

It was most odd, as none of the horses would turn a hair at tractors, trailers, lorries or low flying aeroplanes, but a pony and trap which a hundred years ago would have been the norm threw them completely! To a horse danger is the unfamiliar.

Chapter 15

"Mr. Smith the Blacksmith"

Blacksmiths come in all shapes and sizes, but the first one I knew had his smithy in the centre of a village, and his name was Mr. Smith. He was a short stocky man, with massive shoulders and he was renowned for having a terrible temper if crossed. He had his friends and his enemies living close by, and he also had a very beautiful daughter of whom he was immensely proud.

In those days the village not only had a smithy, but a church, a chapel, a baker who baked long crusty loaves five days a week, and a local squire.

The village consisted of two roads, Main Street and Back Street, and alleyways criss-crossed between the two. In these jitties stood two shops and many houses, in one of which lived Mr. Smith. The alley leading to his house was narrow, but just wide enough for a car to drive up to his door. Three days before his daughter was to be married, he woke up to find a large post set in concrete in the middle of the alley, just where a taxi would turn in to collect the blushing bride.

Lace curtains twitched in eager hands and the air turned blue as Mr. Smith roared with rage and shook his fists to heaven. Meanwhile his daughter wept within the house, and wouldn't come out.

A short while later the village saw the blacksmith stumping up Main Street, past the church and in through the iron gates of the Big House, where he found the owner pottering around admiring his rose beds.

"Squire," said Mr. Smith, "Is there any law that says as I can't remove a post what has been put in where it shouldn't be? And one what is stopping my daughter from getting to her very own wedding."

The Squire rubbed the end of his nose with his hand, and looked at the angry blacksmith:

"No law that I know of," he replied. "After all, if it should not be there, then you cannot be had up for having it shifted, can you." He wished him luck with the forthcoming nuptials, and turned back to his roses.

Mr. Smith stumped back past the church, down Main Street, and stopped at the entrance of the alley, in front of the concrete post. He spat on his hands, braced his knees, and wrapped his strong arms round the obstruction. The muscles on his shoulders bulged, the lace curtains twitched, and he started to pull. At first nothing seemed to happen, and then with a grinding noise and a sudden crack the post rose up high into the air. The blacksmith hefted it in his brawny arms, strode angrily up the jitty, and hurled the offending post straight through the lace clad window of his neighbour. He then dusted his hands down the sides of his cord trousers, and marched triumphantly in through his front door.

By the time the wedding took place three days later the window had been repaired, and the village taxi, draped in white ribbons, swept up to Mr. Smith's door. Miss Smith the Blacksmith's daughter was married in style, and all the villagers except for one, attended the wedding.

The next blacksmith I knew shod a freshly broken Prince for the first time, and he ran a small smithy in a hamlet on the side of a hill, overlooking green fields. He was very quiet, never using two words where a grunt would do, and he had infinite patience with a young horse.

Foals do not need shoes, and a horse that is seldom ridden or hacked only on soft ground such as forest paths can sometimes be left unshod, while a half broken horse sometimes has light shoes on its fore feet only. Any animal that is regularly taken on tarmac roads or ridden regularly however, needs its feet trimmed every six weeks, and worn shoes replaced. If this is not done your horse will go lame, so a good blacksmith is very important, and as you do not want to deal with a rearing kicking animal every six weeks, the first few times a horse meets the blacksmith can make a great difference to your life.

The first foal we bred at the farm was called Chrystal, and we used to bring her and her dam Amber into the stable for grooming and handling. To begin with the foal would skedaddle round the stable hiding behind its mother, peering anxiously at us under her long eyelashes, but as she grew more used to being with people, she would allow us to stroke her, and run our hands down her legs. The next stage was to lift up each of her neat little hooves in turn and to tap lightly on the sole with a hoof pick before putting them gently down again. Then when

134

the blacksmith came out to shoe the other horses, he would do the same thing so that Chrystal grew up with no fear of being shod.

We came to know a variety of blacksmiths at the stables, and as a horse is only as good as its feet, a good farrier was worth his weight in gold. Sometimes a pony would arrive at the farm, hobbling along like an old lady with bunions, and you would find that its hooves had grown so long that they had curved upwards like horns, and split, and it would take ages to repair and heal the feet so that it could be ridden again.

There are occasional exceptions and once we had a large brood mare on loan, called Queenie, who had produced a foal each summer for years but had never been shod. Her hooves had grown as hard as iron, and gave her no trouble at all as long as they were occasionally trimmed.

This process was like trying to carve granite, and she had little feeling in her feet atall. I found this out one busy morning when she trod heavily on my right foot in the yard, and didn't even notice. My poor squashed toes felt as if they were on fire , and I thumped her on the ribs and bellowed my head off, but she merely took another wisp of hay from the haynet and continued to chew happily away.

It was four solid minutes before I could shift her, and I danced around the tarmac in agony before limping away to apply first aid. The same foot was also trampled on one afternoon by Prince, but on that occasion I knew I had to drive back ten miles to the steading. This time both the air and my foot turned purple, and in desperation I crammed a

"Queenie took another wisp of hay."

whole handful of extra strong peppermints into my mouth on the principle that if my mouth was burning, I wouldn't notice the pain in my accelerator foot.

Prince was the lead horse on most hacks, as he was fast and a delight to ride, but occasionally he went lame, and usually the reason was a bruised foot, which required the urgent attention of both vet and blacksmith.

All the horses were checked over every morning to make sure that they were fit, and if there was any doubt in our minds we would walk and trot them back and forth on the hard ground to make sure that they wre sound. One morning Prince did not look happy: he was favouring his near fore and pointing his toe towards the ground, and his head was drooping. When he trotted his action was dot and go one, and he was not happy with himself at all.

We could see no sign of a cut or damage anywhere so we sent for our friendly vet, who came out, pressed the hoof with various implements, and explained that Prince must have trodden on a stone or loose nail. This had bruised the sole of his foot: the bruise had gone inward and become infected and caused a build up of pus inside the hollow box of the hoof. This kind of injury is agonising to a horse as the pressure builds up and the whole foot starts to throb and grow hot to the touch, and unless it is treated the whole hoof can be permanently damaged.

First the foot was scrubbed clean. Next the vet picked out a steel scalpel and bending over picked up Prince's near fore, gripping the leg between his knees to keep it still while he worked. Then millimetre by careful millimetre he cut into the sole of the hoof, with his shoulder hard up against the horse's side. Delighted to have his sore hoof off the hard ground, Prince leant heavily on the vet's shoulder, and turning his head round blew gratefully at the back of his neck. As half a ton of horse pressed down against him, our friendly vet gritted his teeth, and sank lower still under the increasing weight, cutting ever more carefully second by second.

"Stand back"
he gasped breathlessly, as the hoof jerked between his hands, and a stream of pus jetted six feet through the air. Prince breathed a deep sigh of relief, and the vet straightened up slowly, looking six inches shorter as he did so.

"Usual treatment: soak the foot in hot water three times a day, and then put on kaolin poultice and bandage, until the heat goes out of it."

I went off to the kitchen to make a cup of coffee, and to heat the poultice up in the microwave, and later, after the vet had gone, we filled a black bucket with hot water and stood Prince's forefoot in it. He stood happily in the stable while we doctored him and made no attempt to take his hoof out of the water.

Wallowing in the attention, Prince let us poultice him and bandage him, stroke him and hang up a hay net, and gave a contented little whinny as we left the stable. He was obviously feeling much better, and it took him at least half an hour to get all the

138

carefully applied bandages off and distribute them in little muddy heaps all round the stall!

As he grew older, either we became better at bandaging, or Prince grew more tolerant, and the bandages would stay on all night. He was a very good patient as if his fetlocks swelled up after a hard day's ride, we used to stand him in four buckets of water at a time, one at each corner, and he would stand there unperturbed, with an expression of bliss on his dapple grey face.

It takes about twelve days poulticing to rid a bruised foot of infection, and then the blacksmith would come out and put on a special shoe. This had a base plate either of light steel to cover the hole until the horn regrew, or if the foot was healing well, a thick leather cover held in place by the shoe, which protected the sole from further bruising, until the foot was completely recovered.

In either case you needed a good farrier, and I always enjoyed the days when he came. We would line up all the horses that needed attention and tether them to the wall of the steading, swopping them over as each was done. The blacksmith used to do cold shoeing, and would bring the shoes ready made for each horse with him ready to put on. Each rusty old shoe would be removed, and the hoof pared down to the correct shape, with one or two v shaped nicks in the toe, before the new horse-shoes were slotted into place. These were then hammered into position with long square headed nails, before the whole hoof and shoe were filled neatly round leaving the foot cleanly shod with new shoe gleaming in the sun, ready for another days hammering on the hard hard roads.

Chapter 16

"Stormy Days"

The first winter we spent at the farm was wet and dismal, but it was not until one evening in early December, that we realised how fiercely the storms could blow across the valley.

Most of the horses were safely battened down in the stables, all except for one black mare who had refused to come in with the others, and had careered off into the windy darkness and over the hill. Her name was Damsel and as the storm rose, we grew increasingly worried about her, and arm in arm for ballast two of us set off with ropes and torches to find her. All along the edge of the stream we stumped, our heads bowed against the lashing rain, and our green wellies sinking into the muddy grass, calling as we went. There wasn't a sign of her down in the dip, so we struggled up the side of the hill into the teeth of the gale, where the long branches of the trees hailed twigs down onto our heads.

As the howl of the wind dropped for a moment, we called again, and were answered by a frightened whinny. Damsel was huddled under an old ash tree, with her back to the storm, shaking all over from cold and fright. We fastened a headcollar on her, and started back to the stables, trying not to fall on the slippery slope of the hill. Once over the brow the full force of the wind hit us and we hung on to Damsel's mane and staggered on, swaying as the gale battered us from side to side. The mare put her head down and walked steadily on pulling us with her until we reached the lee of the steading, where eager hands opened the stable door and pulled us all inside, into the sweet smelling haven of hay and straw and softly breathing horses.

We stood there dripping for a minute or two getting our breaths back, before dashing out into the yard, under the flapping car port roof and into the welcome warmth of the kitchen. Meanwhile Damsel was rubbed down with wisps of straw until she stopped shivering, and given a hot bran mash, before being rugged up and left to settle down for the night.

There was very little snow that first Christmas, but some years the falls were heavy enough to block the exit to the road. Invariably a horse would need medical attention in the middle of the winter season, and our friendly vet would charge down the snowy track at fifty miles an hour, on the principle that if he went fast enough he wouldn't get bogged down in the drifts. Curiously enough his system worked for him, but not for us. We were for ever digging our vehicles out, and driving up and down in the middle of storms to keep the way open.

One bitter night my husband was motoring back through a blizzard, and rang me on the car phone at 2 oclock in the morning:

"Good morning! Are you all awake?" his voice floated cheerfully over the wire.

"Where are you?" I asked sleepily.

"Look out of the window," came the reply.

Still barely awake I peered out over the fields, and sure enough up on the road I could see stationary headlights fanning out over the white show.

"Get the girls, and some shovels: I'm bogged down," he added unnecessarily.

I roared around the house, pulling on warm clothing as I went, and woke up my daughters. Armed with shovels and torches, we trudged out down the paddock and over the stream. It was a long climb up towards the car through a foot of snow, and every now and then my youngest daughter gave a little snore, and appeared to fall asleep on her feet, only to be prodded awake and pushed ahead towards the lights.

At one point I fell flat on my face in the cold whiteness, and looking up found a large Clydesdale mare gazing down benevolently at this midnight intruder. I stood up and leant gratefully against her lovely warm side, and hanging on to her mane hitched a lift as far as the gate, where I left her blowing out white clouds in the icy air.

"What took you so long?" asked my husband as we came up to the car, with its two deep furrows stretching out behind. "I thought you'd got lost!" He was sitting comfortably in the driving seat listening to the radio, looking at peace with the world, and admiring the scenery.

"I had to wake everyone," I replied crossly, looking at the smooth sheet of white lying between the frozen hedges that lined the road head of us.

"Only a hundred yards or so," he said cheerfully

climbing out of the car, and grabbing a shovel. "Come on you two, start digging!" and with that we set to.

Some twenty minutes later we had cleared enough snow to rock the car free, and he started the engine and reversed a few yards, before easing slowly forward and manoeuvering the car towards the entrance to the track. We watched with baited breath as the car seemed to stop at the curve and then with a grinding of gears the lights turned and accelerated down towards the farmhouse, leaving us behind in the darkness.

Still carrying the shovels and torches my daughters charged back over the fields. I returned to the gate and hung on to my hairy escort for balance, before heading back towards the steading. At the farm fence, I bade her a grateful farewell, and she stood there watching as I trod on the snowy bank and slid through three feet of drift into the cold water of the stream. I was very wet and very cross by the time I reached the kitchen, to be greeted by my other half with the words:

"What on earth took you so long?"

That particular winter was long and cold, but we celebrated Hogmanay with champagne and decided that freezing weather was not so bad after all. The following morning, as we emerged bleary eyed to feed the horses, the stand pipe in the car port snapped off with the cold, and the icy water flowed sluggishly out over the concrete yard.

Knowing that no self respecting plumber would emerge from his lair on New Year's Day even if the

143

roads were passable, we had to solve the problem ourselves. The remedy was obvious: a large Bollinger cork was judiciously applied to the offending pipe, and wedged well into position. It worked like a charm. The leak stopped, and the emergency repair held for a month until our plumber came out and replaced the ancient pipe with a shining new attachment. Which only goes to show that Champagne is a useful beverage to keep on tap in the cold winter months!

The last winter that we were at the steading, we were snowed up for a fortnight or more. This never worried me very much as we had ample food for ourselves, winter fodder for the horses, and although the odd tap would freeze up the main water coming into the house always remained unaffected. There was also a large open fire, and any power cuts were brief as the electricity board would turn out in all weathers to restore supplies to farms.

It was very peaceful in the valley when the roads were blocked by snow. There was no noise of distant traffic, and we existed in our own self sufficient little world. Each day as the drifts grew higher, our early footsteps made fresh pathways through the new layers of white, as if we were the only people on that snow bound land.

One morning after our peaceful two weeks of isolation we heard the grumble of a tractor struggling over the far hill, and by the afternoon we could see it rocking back and forth, with its digger rearing high like some ancient dinosaur. At dusk it fell silent, and the next day we saw two snow ploughs at once, one attacking the drifts from the top of the hill, and the other charging up the road from the village. All day they roared back and forth in turn as the gap between them lessened, and by the third day they met at the end of our track, and the road was open. A nearby farmer kindly cleared our track for us and we were again part of the civilized world.

That was the only winter that we were snowed up for more than a couple of days, and the Autumn storms caused us far more havoc. One blustery day in late September there were storm warnings throughout Scotland and as usual we brought in the animals and fastened all doors and window frames as securely as we could. As the gusts grew stronger, the old blue horse box was blown sideways across the yard, and the big double doors on the indoor school rattled and shook as the blasts hit them. I raced across the yard and went into the school by the calf shed and looked up at the rafters above me. I could see a crack of daylight between the wall and the roof, and with every flurry of wind the crack grew wider.

One telephone call and twenty minutes later three very large men arrived from the nearby town, and we tried to fasten down the roofing panels. At one point they were all hanging onto ropes and the blizzard was lifting them up into the air like puppets as the roof rose and fell. Bricks began to crack off the top of the walls from the thump of the heavy panels above and life was getting decidedly danger-ous, so I sent the men home and retired to the stable block, which was out of the main thrust of the blizzard. Half an hour later there was a terrific blast of wind, and a sharp cracking noise as a third of the barn roof lifted up into the air and abseiled seventy feet into the nearby field.

As the fury of the storm died down, we looked at the damage. Apart from the barn roof, our only casualty was the soaked hay store beneath the missing roof and a few tiles off the main house. No-one was hurt, and the only things missing were half a dozen black buckets which had been stacked in the yard, and which had sailed off into the distance, and two broken windows.

Other people were not so lucky. Driving through to St. Andrews the next day, we counted no less than six overturned caravans, looking like stranded turtles as they lay on their backs, and numerous missing chimneys. Lorries had been blown sideways off the roads and lay crazily propped against hedges, and broken trees littered the slopes of the hills.

A loss adjuster came out to see us a day or two later, and cheerfully climbed up a ladder to inspect the damage, telling us that he was run off his feet with claims. Soon our indoor school possessed a shining new roof, to cover our replaced hay store, and life returned to normal. The following Autumn the same thing happened and the roof was again replaced with even stronger ties to hold it in place. After that it stayed in position through anything the weather could throw at it, but I never dared to keep animals in the barn during the Autumn equinox.

We had been lucky in that our flying roof had soared over the top of the groom's caravan which was tucked in behind the barn, and so sheltered

"The simpler inconveniences of life."

from the full force of the wind. The main damage that occurred to this temporary home was caused by something much simpler – a leaking pipe in the bathroom. This had been dripping away for some time, when an indignant groom appeared one morning, to say that she had fallen through the floor as the lavatory had collapsed underneath her at a most inopportune moment. She added that it was not fair of us to laugh, and could I please get it repaired as quickly as possible.

Of all the hazards of farm life, the simpler inconveniences are far more annoying than the major dramas caused by rain, snow or wind!

Chapter 17

"To Everything there is a Season"

There were horses at the farm before we bought it, and to begin with we took over some of the livery ponies from the former owners, and heard some of their stories.

Everyone who has anything to do with animals knows that their lives are ruled by nature, and that the charms of human owners are completely irrelevant when an animal comes into season. Blind instinct takes over and so ensures the continuation of the species. Mares in season are un-predictable and flirtatious, and a loose stallion will travel miles to find a mate, rounding up all unattached mares en route, as they do in the wild.

One day the stallion at the next door farm escaped and went in search of female company. Seeing him advancing across the fields, the groom rushed back to the steading and hurried all the mares and horses into the stables, before ringing the owner to ask him in no uncertain terms to retrieve his four legged property, before someone was injured. While the owner was on his way the baffled stud-horse roamed round the steading looking for the tempting mares, and neighing in frustration, while the stabled mares called longingly back, and uproar reigned. It was a very relieved groom who saw the stallion recaptured and returned back across the fields.

That first Spring at the steading we had two Shetland Sheep Dogs, Trix and her daughter, Shasta, and they looked like half size orange Lassies. Trix came into season with monotonous regularity, but as the farm was fairly isolated, we did not think that we would be troubled by her admirers, and to begin with all was peaceful.

Then, one balmy day in early May, I couldn't find my left hand green wellie boot. I was sure that I had left it in the carport as usual beside its fellow the night before, but it had vanished. Crossly I pulled on one black and one green boot and stumped off to the stables. The following day three boots were missing, one from each pair, together with a right hand shoe.

Forcing a left hand foot into a right hand boot I started to search for the ghostly walkers, and as I looked out over the curve of the front field, there standing upright against the skyline was one lone green wellie. It looked very silly standing there, and by the time I reached it I could see two others, each one placed separately and erect about a hundred yards apart. The shoe turned up later on top of a wall by the edge of the paddock.

With my arms full of footwear I returned puzzled to the farm, just in time to see a black and white shadow slink out of the stable door. Dropping the boots I dashed round the corner to find Randy, the aptly named sheepdog from a nearby farm disappearing into the open door of the horse box. Carefully I shut him in, and went to telephone his owner.

"Randy at work."

KNIGHT

"Have you lost a sheepdog this morning?" I asked.

"He's over there is he;" came a gruff voice over the line. "Shut him in and I'll come and fetch him later."

"Thanks," I replied, adding cautiously, "Do you know anything about disappearing boots?" There was a moment's silence and then the voice said cheerfully:–

"Oh! That's Randy's work alright. He rounds them up like sheep," and the line went dead.

Later that day Randy was collected, but he returned by evening and in fact spent most of the next month either shut in the horsebox, or jumping over my walls with boots in his mouth, in an effort to entice Trix out to play. Sometimes I would see him peering round the corner with longing black eyes and all the time he grew thinner and thinner from the pangs of unrequited love. I grew quite fond of him, as he was never aggressive or noisy, but his value as a sheepdog must have plummeted. Eventually he went off in search of pastures new, and peace returned to the steading.

Trix's daughter Shasta had been sold when a fat round about pup and bought back when the owners decided not to keep her. She returned with a beautifully brushed coat, a very undernourished body and shaking with fright at every sound. Whenever the dustbin men came and she heard the lorry clattering up the road, she would shoot under a chair in the darkest corner of the inmost room, and would lie there shivering with terror for the next twenty four hours. Not even food would tempt her out of her haven, and all coaxing and stroking were of no avail. Sometimes even the clang of a saucepan lid would send her into hiding and it took me six months to calm her into any sort of sensible behaviour. We thought that perhaps she had been shut inside a dustbin at some time, or been otherwise mistreated, and I bitterly regretted having sold her in the first place.

Everything happened to poor Shasta. After she had returned more or less to normality, we were reversing the horsebox round a corner one afternoon, when she ran across the track and caught the tip of her tail beneath one of the tyres. She shrieked like a banshee and as the wheel released her, took off like a greyhound, tail trailing in the dust, straight for the main road.

We hurtled after her, calling and calling her name, but she was insensible to anything but the pain in her back, and was trying to escape from it in the only way she knew, by running. It was at least twenty minutes and a mile and half later before we managed to catch up with her, and take her down to the vet.

Curiously enough after the first hour she did not seem to be in any pain, but she was unable to wag her tail, which drooped sadly between her hind legs, and affected her balance. As the weeks went by it rose centimetre by centimetre to its normal position, but it took three months before the feeling came back and she was able to hold it up again. Of course after that all vehicles became objects of terror to her, and riding in a car caused her to howl continually from the beginning of the journey to the end.

I have always loved Shelties, and when we moved to the farm, we decided to move up one size in sheepdogs and ended up with two Rough Collies, which we called Bumble and Scruff. Bumble arrived first, at five weeks old, which was really much too young to leave her mother. The daffodils were out on the lawn, with their yellow trumpets meeting over the top of her head, and the puppy bumbled around falling over in a roly poly heap every few minutes, which was how she got her name. Scruff came eight months later, after Trix died of old age, and she was black, furry and very clever.

Both dogs used to land up on the bed in the morning while we had a cup of tea, and of course to begin with Scruff was too small to climb up. This worried Bumble enormously, so after trying in vain to encourage the younger puppy to jump up onto the covers, she went over and picked up one of my husband's socks in her mouth. Returning to the bed, she then trailed this over the side, and barked at Scruff, who took the other end of the sock in her mouth and hung on for grim death, while Bumble, bracing her paws on the eiderdown, retreated slowly across my stomach, pulling the puppy up after her.

We were fascinated: every morning this performance took place until Scruffy was strong enough to climb up on her own, and we could only guess that in the wild, dogs would pull younger ones up to places of safety and that this behaviour was instinctive.

One after effect of this is that Scruffy, who has

grown into a large handsome dog, is addicted to socks, and if the wardrobe door is open, she will carefully remove pairs from their shelf to play with, pounce upon and throw up into the air. She has never chewed anything else: chair legs, shoes and carpet slippers are left untouched, but she considers that all socks are her particular property.

Trix was not the only dog to cause problems in Spring. One of the grooms had a young ridgeback bitch called Gretel. It was a handsome animal and very affectionate, but its owner was a little naive and assured me that her dog would never do anything naughty, as it was far too well trained and obedient to her every command. Now one of the riders had a very large yellow labrador dog, with melting golden eyes and a long feathery tail, called Hansel, and one sunny morning when the fields were full of buttercups and you could feel the grass growing, the two met.

It was love at first sight, and away over the paddock ran the pair, bright eyed and bushy tailed and gambolling like lambs, while the deserted groom danced with rage in the stable yard, and her voice grew hoarser and hoarser as she called her dog to heel.

Both dogs reappeared later in the day, and a swift visit to the vet averted the development of cross bred puppies. After this episode the ridgeback was kept firmly in purdah until the danger period was passed, and eventually produced a pure bred litter for its proud owner.

I have always been fond of mongrels, whether cross breeds or Heinz 57s, and for some reason most large mix-ups seem to be part labrador, while the smaller ones appear to be related to terriers. The first cross breed I knew well was called Nero, and he looked like a mix up between a Jack Russell terrier and a fox hound, being white with one large brown spot on his back. He belonged to my Uncle, and rumour had it that every local puppy was sired by him. Certainly there were a large number of spotted white mixtures around.

At that time one lady in the village bred prize Pekinese dogs, which were her pride and joy. These, together with their mistress, were safely ensconced behind a six foot high stone wall on the edge of the main street. One Spring her prize bitch came into season, and the village was informed of the imminent arrrival of future Pekinese show winners. Unfortunately when the litter of pups appeared, some were true to form, being snub nosed and yellow in shape, but there were also a couple of white short coated youngsters with one brown spot each.

The not so proud owner of these mixed up offspring then tried to bring a paternity writ against Nero, although as no-one knew how an aging cross bred terrier could have scaled a six foot wall, she had no success. However for a while passions ran high, and the village enjoyed themselves exceedingly with witty comments on white and yellow canines of uncertain parentage.

The other mix up I knew well was inherited from an elderly Great Aunt and was called Bruce. She had discovered him years before starving in a ditch with a jagged cut in his side and had nursed him back to health.

Despite the traumas of his past he was one of the gentlest dogs I knew. To look at he was large, black and a pleasant mixture of retriever, labrador and spaniel. All in all he was a good looking dog, with a long tail and a silky coat.

When he first arrived we lived in an army quarter in Tidworth and our daughters were only three and four. They spent that first afternoon queueing up at the back door with three small friends, while Bruce sat in state on the kitchen step, shaking paws with each child as it came past. This occupied them all very happily until teatime, and with every hand shake there was a friendly thumping sound from the dog's wagging tail, together with a lop sided grin.

Bruce behaved angelically for a week, until I put him in the back of the car one day and took him shopping. On the way back I saw a friend and blew the horn. Bruce gave a howl and made a flying leap over the passenger seat and onto my lap, where he continued to howl, shivering and shaking with fright, as I hastily pulled into the side of the road.

It took me five minutes to calm him down, and I drove home very slowly, hoping that no-one else would be blowing car horns anywhere near us. It is not easy to drive with an unexpected three stone of hairy mongrel landing between you and the steering wheel, and we could only guess that the poor dog had once been involved in an accident and associated a car horn with past terror.

Something had to be done, and so for a fortnight we drove Bruce to a deserted field once a day and parked there blowing the horn and feeding him on biscuits. Gradually he became used to the noise and didn't bother any more, but he was never very fond of car journeys, and tolerated them only as a necessary prelude to interesting walks.

The other problem Bruce had was that he was firmly convinced that every large dog, whether male of female, was longing for his attentions, and so when other animals were around he had to be kept firmly on a lead.

All dogs have their idiosyncrasies, whether cross bred or pedigreed, but whatever their breeding they have the same inbred characteristics that kept their ancestors alive in the wild. Nature has its own rules.

Chapter 18

"The Big Boys"

The next door farm to ours bred Clydesdales, those great gentle creatures that are rarely seen nowadays except at agricultural shows, when they appear groomed and plaited, with their foot feathers whitened with chalk, and their harnesses gleaming and studded with silver.

Because of their size, the yearlings appear even more long legged and gangly than other foals, and we used to see the young ones harnessed up to a frame and towing bales of hay through the fields to accustom them to pulling weights behind them.

Some of the bigger riding horses have traces of the old style draught horses in their appearance, which gives them heavy feathers round their hooves, and immense strength. We always thought that Brutus had some shire ancestry as he was both powerful and slow, although he could keep going at his own pace for a very long time. He was not however aware of his bulk, and one day when his evening bucket was delayed, he decided to copy the thieving habits of wicked little Shetlands, and raid the feed room, the door of which had been left invitingly open.

Unfortunately the doorway to this gourmet's heaven was narrow and only his head and shoulders passed through, which left his swelling sides firmly stuck between the door posts, and his quivering nostrils two feet from the nearest bin of oats. It was a very frustrated Brutus that was hauled backwards by his mane and returned to his stable, but he didn't try it again, merely casting wistful glances at the feed room door as he passed.

Because he was so broad and heavy, Brutus could carry men up to fifteen stone or more, and was useful on treks. Smaller riders had difficulty in getting their legs round his rotundity, and children would sit on the saddle with their legs straight out as though on a table top. Unlike big Barona who was a good sixteen hands and as gentle as a lamb, Brutus was not really suitable for light weight riders, but he had his admirers.

There was one girl who always seemed to turn up for a two hour ride whenever the weather was bad, and she loved Brutus. Off they would plod, groom in front on a reluctant Barona, with a disgusted Brutus plodding in the rear, rain pouring off their shoulders and dripping down their manes into the mire below. Two hours later they would all return, still plodding, soaked through and splashed with mud, with the groom dying for a cup of tea and hot buttered toast, and the horses dreaming of a hot bran mash and a rub down in a nice warm stable.

We didn't know that Brutus could gallop at all, until one stormy day during a ride when there was a thunderclap and lightning struck a tree sixty yards away. Away Brutus charged, followed pell mell by the other scared horses, and once going he was difficult to stop. On and on he lumbered, heading for

"Stuck in the feed room door"

161

home and the safety of his green field, and where he led the others followed. They couldn't pass him as his bulk filled the walled track, so they all cantered along in line behind him until he finally came to a stop, and order was restored.

I seldom rode, mainly because my favourite horses were always being ridden, and one fine afternoon my eldest daughter coaxed me into exercising Brutus in the field. It was not a happy experience. No sooner was I in the saddle, than the normally placid horse took off at a hand gallop, and went into a series of fifteen bucks in a row, with me bouncing around like a pumpkin on top and swearing blue murder. It took me a hundred yards to pull him up and get some sense into him, and I was furious at this freakish behaviour, which was completely out of character for this normally stolid gelding. It reminded me yet again that even the most placid of animals can behave unpredictably.

Apart from the odd bruised foot, Brutus was very healthy, but one winter morning I went into the stables to check the horses and found a very unhappy horse, standing with his head drooping and his neck turned round as if he was admiring his off hind fetlock. He seemed unable to straighten up and would not eat his food, which was unheard of, as Brutus was normally the greediest of all the horses. Fearing that he might have injured himself by getting cast in the stable we sent for the vet, to see if he could be folded back to his normal four square position with a leg at each corner, and a head in front.

Out came our local lady vet, who although

blessed with a marvellous disposition, and numerous Jack Russell terriers, was not overtall. She stood in the stable and looked at Brutus, who leered sideways at her out of his left eye, but remained firmly stuck. After a pain killing injection, which perturbed him not at all, Brutus slowly swung his head round to the correct end, but remained lopsided with his right ear pointing strawwards.

"Ear trouble" said the vet briskly, as she gazed up at one side of Brutus' large head, and added "I'll need a chair."

Eager hands carried a chair through to the stable and she climbed up onto it. This had the result of bringing her face level with the afflicted ear, and I was worried that one fling of Brutus' great neck would send her flying. Not a bit of it. Brutus stood like a wry necked statue, while the vet gently poked, prodded and examined the afflicted ear, murmuring quietly to the horse as she did so. Finally she put in drops, and climbed down again with a smile.

"Apply the drops three times a day," she instructed, "and let me know if he doesn't improve rapidly."

Off she went complete with canine escort, and over the course of the next day Brutus's head gradually returned to a horizontal position. He remained unmoved by the application of drops, merely tipping his head sideways as if to help, and was in every way a model patient. As I said animals can be unpredictable.

Most big horses like companionship, and many travel with a stable mate who acts as a tranquilliser. I know of one stallion who was kept calm by a rabbit in its stall, and many horses will happily go to sleep with a cat curled up in the straw beside them. Others however, have odder companions, and one night when several show jumpers were staying at the stables I went out to check them all last thing before going to bed.

As usual I was greeted with little whinnies, and blown at over the stable doors, but there was also an unexpected sound, a bleat.

Startled, I peered over the half door, and there in the corner of the stall, side by side with this majestic eighteen hand bay, was a small white goat. It looked back at me, and bleated again, before rubbing its head affectionately against the flank of its stable mate. The big horse slumbered peacefully on, unworried by the strange surroundings, while its guardian angel kept watch beside him .

A group of horses will protect each other from aggression, and are wary of newcomers. There was a chestnut gelding called Russet, who was a bully. He had a very bad habit of biting, although we did not know this when he joined us. Russet did not bite people, but he used to sneak up behind another horse and bite hard just above the root of its tail.

Oddly enough the attacked animal never kicked, but tried to escape with little jumps and wriggles of the hind quarters, so that the two horses would proceed round the field as if they were doing an offbeat conga. His usual target was Kingston, who had no idea how to retaliate, but Russet would also bite any horse smaller than himself when he thought he could get away with it.

This was finally stopped by the other horses, who

were becoming tired of being bitten and had obviously decided that Russet should be taught a lesson. One afternoon just as he had sneaked up behind Kingston, and opened his mouth to bite at his victim's rear end, Prince came up behind Russet, and in turn bit hard at Russet's tail. Kingston shot off leaving Russet facing the fence, and at the same moment the two biggest horses, Brutus and Barona came up one each side of Russet and shouldered into his sides.

He was well and truly caught. He could move neither forward nor back, and every time he tried to shift to the side, Brutus and Barona held him in place. In vain did Russet wriggle and squeal. Prince continued biting and the three avengers held him there for a solid twenty minutes, before slowly moving away and letting him go.

I hauled Russet into the stable and applied first aid, and it was a very sore and sorry horse that returned to the field, with a large patch of purple spray adorning his rump. He retired to a corner and stayed there with his head hanging for two days, while the other horses studiously ignored him. He was in disgrace, and he knew it. Kingston trotted around looking very smug, and after this episode, Russet never bit another horse. The newcomer had been put in his place, and gave no more trouble.

One of the heaviest horses we had at livery was Queenie, the brood mare, who had a large broad back, and who was even harder than Brutus to wrap your legs around. She was very placid, and would allow you to do anything with her, but she was rather like a tank, in that once started in one direction, she was difficult to stop. She also had a habit of strolling through fences as if they were not there, leaving a trail of broken posts and tangled wires behind her.

Jupiter was another of the big horses, and stayed with us for a while before being sold by his owner. He was beautiful to look at, bright chestnut in colour and very young. Overcome by his beauty, his proud possessor called him various names, and no sooner had the horse come to answer to Jupiter, than he was rechristened Apollo, Oberon or Zeus, or some other name equally suitable to his appearance. After the third change in as many weeks, we reverted to calling him Jupiter, to which he answered quite happily about ten percent of the time.

None of this worried the animal in the slightest, as he was too busy being alive to care what he was called. Anything interesting in the distance was an immediate attraction, and he would set off full of curiosity, eyes set on his goal, regardless of what lay in his way. Gates, whether open or shut, were a matter of sublime indifference to his majestic bulk, as were wire fences, rails or stable doors, or anything below eye level. Full of curiosity, Jupiter made straight for his goal, leaving a path of havoc behind, and I was very glad when he moved on, beautiful though he was.

The first thoroughbred horse I ever rode was a black mare called Witch, and she belonged to a Great Aunt of mine, who hunted sidesaddle until she was well into her seventies. Her back remained straight as a wand, and she rode as if she were part centaur. Dressed in a sweeping black habit she would career off over the Dorset downs, accompanied by an equally elderly lady dressed in green, called appropriately enough, Miss Hunt.

Only when she had ridden for two hours, would I be allowed to take Witch out, and apart from one occasion the mare behaved impeccably. That time a heath fire blow up in the gorse behind me and Witch galloped headlong for safety, while I bounced up and down on the sidesaddle facing left and clinging on for dear life. It seemed a very long time before we came to a stop, and it was a long way home, and after that I decided that riding astride was much more comfortable, as at least the bruises afterwards were placed symmetrically.

I never knew which I loved most, the big boys or the little ponies with their mischievous ways, but there is something about the seventeen or eighteen hand horses that is lacking in the smaller animals. They are big; most of them are gentle to handle, and usually they are easier to ride. They are also marvellous company.

Chapter 19

"The Age of Elegance"

Horses can be beautiful, but looking after them is not an elegant existence. It is not only physically hard work, but it can be dangerous, and people who muck out stables do not smell of Chanel No 5.

Our manure heap at the farm had a rich life of its own. In summer when it was at its most odoriferous, we would have numerous eager faced gardeners appearing in the yard. Their green fingers would be atwitch with anticipation, and their eyes would swivel longingly towards the steaming mass.

"Could you let us have some manure for the roses? Just two or three sacks would do."

They would look longingly towards the smelly pile as if it were black gold, and I would wave them benignly on and hand them some old feed bags.

"Help yourself," I would say cheerfully. "You'll find a fork by the fence."

Some of them would beam happily back, grab the fork and start filling the sacks, before dumping them reverently in the boots of their cars and driving off down the track with bootcover and all windows open. Others would visibly flinch, and after dabbing at the muck with its attendant flies for a minute or two would retire, handkerchiefs to quivering noses, with enough muck to feed about one small tea-rose.

We were very happy to give away manure, as in hot weather the over heated straw sometimes caught fire from internal combustion, and trails of smoke would rise slowly heavenwards, until parts of the pile smouldered away to black ash. In autumn it grew toadstools, and increased in size as more horses were stabled, and the farm cats were often to be found curled up there in cold weather, cosily asleep on top of their own central heating plant.

Our muck heap not only had its admirers, it was examined annually by inspectors, as part of the environmental health regulations concerning riding stables and farms. Each year we would be told to improve its position or build a soak away or a drainage pit, and each year this was postponed as being impractical, unnecessary or too expensive.

In any case, part of the time the heap did not exist as the mushroom farmers used to come and pay us to let them take it away. Their year round crops seemed to need an unending supply of fresh dung, preferably from horses, and suitably mixed with good wheat straw, and just when we were reaching the stage of not being able to reach the top of the heap, their lorry would arrive complete with huge orange grab, and remove the lot.

One day when we were stacking up the muck heap, a strange blue van drove into the yard. That August there had been numerous thefts of saddlery from stables in the area, and we were becoming increasingly wary of strange vehicles and unwelcome visitors. My daughter and I approached cautiously from the rear of the vehicle, with our pitchforks at the ready.

Slowly the driver's door opened, and out stepped a medium sized man in a blue uniform. He looked at us, and flinched visibly, his nostrils aquiver, as I enquired politely as to what he wanted. Wordlessly, with his hand shaking, he took a pass from his pocket and held it out for me to examine . It turned out that he was an inspector who came round to see that farms were fulfilling all health and safety regulations, so we put down our weapons, and retired to the kitchen for a soothing cup of tea. We must have appeared far more menacing than we were.

Odd vans and lorries used to appear regularly at the farm in search of scrap metal, or looking for tracks to tarmac. One man appeared twice yearly, in April and September, with a load of new gates in the back of a trailer. These came in two sizes, and arrived with the paint still wet. Sometimes they were silver grey, and once they were rusty red, and they came complete with heavy hangers to attach them to the gateposts.

It took a long time to buy a gate, as the purchase involved much leaning on fences and a slow amicable bargaining session, usually ending with a cup of coffee, and the propping of the new gate against the wall to await erection.

In the long summer holidays students would come looking for casual work, or on the hottest days of all the sewer men would roll up in their tanker and clean out the cess pit. As the farm was not on main drainage, this had to be done twice yearly, and in winter the pipes leading from the stables invariably froze and became blocked. They also caused problems in summer when the dust

170

clogged the runnels, and the only cure was a fifty yard long piece of heavy rubber hose. This lived behind the indoor school, and weighed a ton, as did the manhole covers which dotted the ground at intervals.

The trick was to raise all the covers and block them open with crowbars, before feeding the heavy pipe from hole to hole and pumping it back and forth as hard as you could. This necessitated bracing your legs, and heaving the long hose up and down for about ten minutes. At the same time you ran water down the drains until with a flatulent whoosh the whole smelly blockage cleared itself and hiccuped away. It was a very messy procedure and required old clothes, disinfectant, and a hot bath afterwards. It also made one very cross.

One very warm day when I had just tidied myself up after clearing a particularly obstinate blockage, an immaculate grey car drove gingerly up the track and into the yard, weaving between the potholes as it came.

Out climbed an extremely well dressed lady, freshly set hair lacquered to her head, and dainty heeled shoes on her long and slender feet. She looked very elegant and very out of place as she stepped warily over the black pipe, and we retired to the kitchen to talk.

After some conversation it turned out that she had a young horse that she wanted kept for her daughter Jane, who would be coming to ride during the school holidays. This pony was a recent acquisition, as her husband had disappeared and

171

left her on her own, and she thought that it would be a new interest for her.

So often we found that one parent families would rush out and buy a pet for their child, as if to compensate for the missing father or mother. In some cases it seemed to help: but in others it just led to vast livery bills being sent to the absent partner, and the horse becoming part of a tug of war between the two factions, or being sold in a hurry when money ran short. I would find children weeping their hearts out behind the hay bales, and although my heart ached for them, there was no cure for what they were suffering, except to help them to accept things and to come to terms with the upheavals in their young lives.

However, when Jane arrived to ride, she was a bouncy happy individual, who took the world in her stride, and had enormous fun on her six year old chestnut pony. Her Mother would come sometimes to watch, but as she informed me that she rested and did her embroidery after lunch, we did not see much of her. In her world as she put it,

"Doesn't everyone do tapestry work in the afternoons?"

I had a great admiration for the well turned out people of the horse world. A horse and rider doing dressage is a work of art just as much as a beautiful painting, and a perfectly plaited mane takes a lot of practice before it looks right. It is also great fun to do, and was one of the skills that we used to teach visiting children. Various patterns suit different types of mane, and it is necessary to have a large supply of plastic bands and a coarse needle and thread to match the colour of the hair. If you are not very tall, you will also need a bucket to stand on, and it is hard on the hands, If you are not careful you end up with numerous small cuts, but the end result is very satisfying, and if properly done will last for the two or three days.

We used to plait up our horses before gymkhanas, and they looked very attractive, but one of my favourites at the shows were the big Clydesdales.

As these big animals paraded round the ring with their blue ribbons, burnished hooves and ornamental collars they were like a moving portrait from a slower age, when man and beast worked together to make a living from the land. As a child in Dorset, I used to see pairs of the Shire horses with one man behind, ploughing the fields and I never tired of watching their slow dignity. There was a sense of harmony and a pattern in the changing seasons, as they repeated themselves each year, and people seemed to have more time for each other.

These days no-one seems to have time, and the tractors and vast combines clatter and bang their way through the fields, and no doubt the ploughmen who walked behind their horses through the sodden plough, with aches in their legs and rheumatism in their backs would have found modern mechanisation a blessing.

Horses however, need a great deal of looking after, and some of the mothers and children took infinite pains in preparing their miniature steeds for shows, and would arrive at first light to start grooming and polishing their already gleaming ponies.

One day a family turned up with a brand new show blanket tastefully edged with petunia piping, and decorated with the pony's name, while the mother's fingernails were painted to match. I was very glad when the rider came out with the usual pastry brush and started to anoint her mount's hooves with the normal coloured black hoof oil, as I had a mental vision of the pony's feet being dyed to match the ensemble.

Caring for horses means very different things to different people, and it is possible to spend a fortune on accessories and riding gear. Some of the riders used to turn up dressed like models, on the principle that if you looked the part, it was easier to ride. Unfortunately it did not work like that, and it is better to learn to ride, and make sure that you like the sport before spending the earth on equipment.

Children can learn to ride in jeans and hard shoes, provided they have a hard hat, and most stables will provide these for hire. Jodhpurs and riding breeches are certainly more comfortable to ride in, and they help, as do riding boots, but there is a thriving second hand market in these, and as children grow so fast, it is worth investigating the cheaper possibilities.

We always kept a few spare pairs of jodphurs or breeches at the farm for visiting children who used to come on the summer courses, as it was a little hard if all the others were beautifully turned out and they had only jeans to wear. However, many riders managed to equip themselves very inexpensively, and one of the odd things was that at the end of the season we would find we had more spare pairs of boots and jodhpurs than we started with, and despite putting notices up very few of them were ever reclaimed.

I suppose, that like umbrellas abandoned in railway carriages, people forgot where they had left them, but I often thought that there must have been alot of cold people walking around Fife with their legs and feet bare.

Keeping horses is a life of contrasts: one day you are elegantly dressed and on show to the world, and the next you are knee deep in muck, covered with flies and shifting deep litter out of stables. Whatever happens, you are very rarely bored.

Chapter 20

"Water, where are you?"

There are many lovely places to live in this island of ours, but the farm we had in Scotland was one of the loveliest. Set in a wide sweeping valley with the nearest house half a mile away, we lived in our own world.

There are drawbacks to country living in that buses are few and far between, but if you keep horses and dogs and incidentally children it is a very satisfying way of life.

In remote areas mains services are sometimes non existent, or unreliable, but our farm was on mains electricity. The water however came from a hill spring, and then flowed in a stream down a slope to a holding tank, with sticklebacks in the outlet pool, and from there to the steading opposite.

If a tractor ploughed too deep in the wrong place it would sever the pipe, and the long suffering plumber would be called out to repair it. Unlike town plumbers, ours came equipped with waders, and possibly gills.

The first time this happened was in spring when the ground was just beginning to thaw. I had been happily watching a tractor ploughing on the other side of the valley. Clouds of birds were wheeling behind the tracks and settling on the new turned earth, like children at a school picnic. I was feeling happily rural and content with my life, until I went to draw some water for Janie the Shetland.

When the tap in the stables was turned on, it usually gave three hiccups and a belch and then gushed out with enough force to drench unwary bucket fillers. This area of the farm was definitely wellie boot land, but this time there was only a sucking noise, a deep sigh and a solitary drip of water at the end of the spout.

After trying various other taps I climbed up to the attic, and found the main tank half empty, and the incoming pipe dry. The supply came onto the farm through a black pipe over the stream, and once before when the pressure had dropped, I had traced the leak by the simple process of crawling along the ground and listening to the flow, as the pipe ran only a few inches below the surface.

All this had taken a while, so by the time I had driven over to the nearby farm, the tractor had finished and gone. Wandering round the deserted buildings, I found a large pool on the edge of the freshly ploughed field, with water bubbling up in the middle, and little wavelets rippling gently against the furrows.

Out came our disgruntled plumber, and armed with waterproofs and the inevitable waders, he stepped gingerly out into the centre of the spreading pond. He was not a happy man. It took twenty four hours to reconnect the pipe, which was then left standing up on a brick base as a warning signal to future marauding tractors.

In the meanwhile, a kindly farmer from the top of the hill brought us some large white containers of fresh water for the house, and we turned the horses out to drink from the stream at the edge of the paddock, and filled any necessary buckets from this ever flowing source.

Despite these odd leaks, the water was of beautiful quality. Unlike town water, which to me resembles chlorinated cardboard, it tasted alive, and although the pressure dropped a little in hot weather, this was probably due to cattle being watered nearby, and we had very little trouble with the supply.

According to the dowsing rods, there was also a pool of water under the top end of the calf shed, and I never knew if this was another underground spring, or an old well. It could have been part of an old land drain, as every field had a stream on one side of it, and the ground was clay.

One advantage of highland spring water is that it makes delicious wine. Also in Scotland there are vast areas of growing raspberries, where you can pick your own. Put the two together and you had a marvellous drink, which improved with keeping. The hard part lay in hiding the finished wine away from the family, who had little interest in waiting for it to mature.

Recently in Wales, I found a dozen bottles of the 1985 vintage stacked away under the stairs where it had been dumped when we moved in. Full of delight we tried it and its six year rest had turned it into a beautiful rose coloured drink, with a slight sparkle and definite cheering qualities.

At the farm I used to make wine from everything in season, and twelve gallons would be bubbling happily away in different parts of the steading, according to the temperature required. I used one gallon hens in preference to larger demijohns, as they were easier to move around.

Years before, full of enthusiasm over my new hobby, I had started a five galloner of elderberry only to find that I had no cork large enough to fit the neck of the bottle. As there had been a recent children's birthday party, there were various surplus balloons lying around, and full of ingenuity, I slipped a bright blue one over the top as substitute air lock, and fastened it down with orange baling twine. It looked very tasteful.

All went well for a day, and the balloon filled a little, and was lying limply hanging down as I went to bed. During the night I woke up and went to make a cup of tea, to find that the balloon was now about two feet in diameter, vibrating gently, and tight as a drum.

Carefully I released one side of the balloon and a great whoosh of alcohol ridden air rushed out into my face. Fascinated I replaced my makeshift valve and watched as it slowly started to refill. Three times that night I let out the surplus gases and returned to bed, and the following morning made a hasty expedition into town for a cork of suitable size, and a new and better airlock. I needed my sleep.

That was a good year for wine, and I made not only strawberry and elder, but blackberry, rosehip and peach, with a few gallons of apple mixed in.

Elderberry always seemed temperamental, and one year before we moved to the farm, I had thirty six bottles stacked on shelves in a downstairs bathroom.

Being an optimist I had thought that they would do well there, and being a practical person, I had stored them facing the bath, so that if their corks exploded, the resultant tide of wine would have a safe landing place. Unfortunately the weather was very hot, and one morning I went in to find the bath littered with corks and the floor awash with purple elderberry wine. Not only did it take ages to clear up, but it stained the cream linoleum permanently pink, so after that I abandoned elderberry wine as being too hot to handle.

At the farm the second stage of fermentation used to take place in the shelved understair cupboard, which I had wallpapered and used as an ironing station. It was very peaceful in there with the airlocks pop popping away, and the glup glup noise made a soothing background to the ironing of husband's shirts. The fumes were sometimes quite potent, and on warm days great wafts of wine would permeate the dining room every time the cupboard door was opened and I would emerge from my lair, laden with a neat pile of laundry, and a beatific expression.

The reason why the wine making was so successful was the quality of the water, and to us there was a definite advantage in not being connected to the mains.

When I was a child in Dorset, again we were on a private supply, which dwindled and died if a nearby duck pond was being filled, or someone left a tap running. We also had our own generator for electricity, which chugged away at the back of the garage, and provided lighting, and the cautious use of an electric toaster. Pressing clothes was done in the kitchen by flat irons heated up on the stove, and heating came from a solid fuel boiler and open fires. If I was cold at night, I used to pull up a dog or an extra blanket.

It all seemed to work very well, except on one occasion when a friend of mine came to stay, and the toaster was left on overnight by mistake. The lights then grew very dim, and at the same time the water supply faded away, and we had to clean our teeth in soda water by the light of a hurricane butty. The toothpaste tasted disgusting and my friend did not come and stay again.

Wherever we have lived, we seem to have had trouble with pipes. In Durham where we lived for several years, we were on mains water, and our problems were largely self inflicted.

Attached to the cottage where we lived was a large dilapidated green house some thirty feet long, which formerly had not only electric light, but also a powerful heating system, and taps. When we discovered that this meant that the building was rated as domestic, we decided to save money and pull it down, and invested in a sledge hammer and ladder.

All went well until my husband fell off the ridge of the green house into the horse radish plants. He was unhurt but indignant, and proceeded to take the building down carefully piece by piece, ending up by digging out the earth floor to make a vegetable patch.

One Saturday evening as he attacked the packed earth, his sharp spade sliced neatly through the water main, and an elegant plume of crystal liquid fountained into the air. Getting a plumber on a weekday is not always easy, and weekends are even more difficult. This time it took until Monday to repair the leak, and we had to go round to the local doctor next door, who was on the same intake pipe, and warn him that he would have to have his evening whisky neat.

As a small child during the war, the rented house we had in an Oxfordshire village, was blessed with wisteria round the door, an acacia tree in the front garden and an intermittent water supply. The same underground spring served both us and the shoemaker opposite, and if one house had water the other ran short. People were always trotting crossly across the road carrying buckets, and each house had its own pump. Ours stood some six feet tall at one side of the scullery, and was painted a a lurid shade of green. Its long curving handle had to be worked by hand, and every morning there was a dawn race to see who could get their supply in first. I was not big enough to help, and for me these early morning aerobics were only a spectator sport.

It was a time of water conservation. A large bottle had to be kept in the lavatory cistern to reduce the amount drawn, and bath water was limited to three inches, and recycled onto the rose beds and vegetable garden. Once I put potassium permanganate in the bath to turn it purple and make life more interesting, and was sent to bed supperless in disgrace.

That year my Grandfather had a wonderful display of lupins. In serried ranks they rose, in pink and red and blue and yellow, their plumes marching in dainty columns across the flower borders, while roses climbed the trellises above. All these flowers needed my bath water to survive, and led me into more trouble, as at that time we had a guest staying who was not very popular, and who had stayed with us for a very long time.

That summer I had been taken to a wedding in the village church, and had watched with awe as confetti had been thrown over the bridal pair, and it had been explained to me that this was done as a sign of rejoicing. When our guest finally departed, I thought that this also was a matter for rejoicing, and having no confetti, I carefully went out into the garden early and stripped all the lupins of their many coloured petals, and to show how especially joyful the occasion was, I also pulled the petals off any roses I could reach.

Then, when the guest was saying her protracted farewells at the front door, with little murmurs about returning soon, before catching the early train, I climbed up on the porch above, and rained the fragrant petals down upon her head, shouting out "Allelluia" as I did so.

She did not appreciate my well meaning efforts, and yet again I was banished to bed, in even deeper disgrace because of the ruined flowers. However my Grandfather quietly slipped tuppence into my hand as a reward, and said that it was worth it, so I was not unhappy.

My Mother made elderberry wine that year, and stored the finished bottles in the cellar. It was during the time of air raid warnings, and bangs in the night, and when in the dead vastness of the blackout, a series of explosions shook the house, everyone was convinced it was bombs, and rushed for shelter.

It was not until first light the next morning that we found a cellar swimming in wine, broken bottles flung in every direction, and corks everywhere. That particular spring water must have had a kick like a mule.

Chapter 21

"Animal Grab"

Anyone who keeps animals, will at some time have to take part in a game of animal grab. Like small children, most animals want to be free, while their owners want them safely under control.

The first mass escape I saw was in a village called Steeple Aston, where my family bred Chinchilla and Blue Rex rabbits. A large buck rabbit gnawed through the corner of his cage during the night, and went round overturning all the runs in the orchard, including those containing the litters and their does.

In the morning there were fifty two bunnies running loose. A couple of chinchillas were playing on the lawn, while others were hopping around the rosebeds. The blue rex buck and his relatives were happily munching their way through the rows of carrots, and three of the young ones were playing tig among the potatoes. Some of the babies had fallen asleep among the lettuces, and the large buck rabbit who had caused all this mayhem was discovered in the front seat of the car, peering out through the open window, and looking very pleased with himself.

This was animal grab in earnest. It took us three days to round them up and replace them securely back in their runs and cages, and even then two had disappeared completely, either victims of a fox or on permanent walk about. One or two of the does looked a little confused for a while, as some of their offspring had been exchanged during the round up, but in the end they all settled down amicably enough after their outing, in their reinforced cages. They had obviously enjoyed the unaccustomed exercise.

Nearby there was a field called the Dene, which had a mass of mixed black and white and brown rabbits living in a vast warren running up the side of a hill. After our great escape, there were probably some long coated or blue grey ones to add to the general colour scheme.

As it was wartime, we also kept eleven goats, which supplied us with milk, and they were great escapologists. A white nanny went missing from the orchard one day, and was discovered in the dining room licking out the marmalade pot, and another nanny goat called Miranda was a great climber of apple trees. Many of these were old, with sloping trunks, and Miranda used to stroll up to the first branches and then lie down, hidden by leaves, while she thoughtfully chewed up any apple she could reach. She was particularly fond of orange pippins, and she would remain there in her shady refuge peering at us through the low branches as we rushed around trying to find her.

Occasionally one or more of the herd would chomp through their tethers, jump over a wall and go adventuring, and we would have to retrieve them from nearby orchards or fields. They were not

"Licking out the marmalade pot."

easy to catch unless it was near milking time, when they were more co-operative, and they seemed to treat our efforts as a huge joke. As well as being very smelly, goats have a definite sense of humour, and a vast curiosity about everything.

The Billy spent part of his time in a stable, and whenever anything of interest happened there would be a loud clattering, and his fore legs and wagging beard would appear inquisitively over the half door. There he would remain, his eyes avidly fixed on any passing nanny goat, dog or cat, until they were out of sight, when he would retire from view, to reappear in an instant at the sound of footsteps.

At other times he was tethered down by the stream at the end of the orchard, from where he could keep an eye on his numerous relatives. Unlike his wives, he made no attempt to run away, and if he slipped his tether, would lie down beside it, or wander peacefully back to his stable.

After the war my parents moved to Dorset, minus goats, but with dogs and ducks and hens instead.

The house we lived in then was edged on two sides by woods, and on the other two by a golf course and open fields, with a rough track running along the edge of the nearest pasture. It was fairly isolated, with the nearest cottages a mile away down the bottom of a long steep hill.

We kept both ordinary sized hens which were Rhode Island Reds, and a dozen very pretty Bantams, but the respective cock birds lived in a permanent state of war, and their main aim in life was to get through the wire fencing and kill each other. It is not easy to separate fighting cocks, and in the end we had to dispose of the big cockerel, because he would attack anything that came near his hens, including his owners, and we were getting tired of having to fight him off with a broom whenever we entered the run.

The Bantam cock was delighted at the disappearance of his rival, and crowed with triumph every morning at dawn, but it meant that the big hens had lost their protector, and were more vulnerable to attack.

At Christmas time as the season of goodwill spread over Dorset, so did the chicken thieves. Every run within miles of us had been raided, and some people had lost all their birds. This always happened on dark nights, when there was no moon.

At the time when the chickens were vanishing, we had a spaniel called Freckles, and an eight month old Alsatian puppy called Zariah. She was at the long leggedy stage and very nervous, and when she barked, it was from sheer fright. However to anyone who did not know how young she was it sounded very deep toned and menacing, and she would growl under her breath if anyone came near the house after dark.

Before going to bed one night, Zariah growled and leaning out of the window I heard footsteps moving along the track. There was a mutter of voices, and I grabbed Zariah and tiptoed down the garden parallel with the walkers, heading for the edge of the wood, where our hens were kept. Zariah pattered along beside me, my hand on her collar, but she did not make a sound.

When we reached the hen runs, I could hear voices the other side of the wall, and there was a sound of boots scraping against the stone. Nudging the dog, I said in as deep a voice as I could,

"Who goes there!" and at the same moment Zariah started to bark. She sounded very fierce indeed.

There was a hurried muttering from beyond the wall, a clank of metal, and then the sound of fleeing footsteps on the soft earth.

Zariah and I were very pleased with ourselves, as the raiders did not return, and ours were the only chickens that survived into the New Year. The next day I found an abandoned crowbar at the base of the wall.

A troop of gipsies used to appear in the area about three times a year, and they were a hardy lot. Once in December, when there was snow on the ground and ice on the puddles, I saw them sleeping out in the open round a camp fire, oblivious of the weather, and I often wondered if they were the hen rustlers.

In September, when the golf course in front of the house was covered with wild mushrooms, you had to get up at first light in order to find any for breakfast as the gipsies used to camp nearby and pick them for the market. As the mushrooms finished, so did the gipsies vanish overnight. One day they would be there, and the next there would be no sign of them except the cold ashes of their fires, and the slivers of wood left over from their hand made clothes pegs.

It was a good area for mushrooms, and often I would go searching for them in the fields behind the woods, with Zariah and my spaniel Freckles for company.

There was one grass field which had a deep valley through the centre of it, and two great bomb craters. These were overgrown and a hiding place for hares. Each time we went Zariah would race the hares, and her flying grey form would speed over the grass in chase, but she never caught them. If she stopped for breath, the hares would stop also, and sit up watching her until she started after them again. They certainly had no fear, as they were far faster than she was, and knew every hiding place in the rough ground and brambles that rimmed the craters.

Near the edge of the field up against the thick thorn hedges, were several fairy rings of mushrooms, and once in the early morning, I was happily picking these for breakfast, when up over the side of the valley came the most enormous black bull I had ever seen. As he saw me he quickened his pace and then came to a halt about twenty yards away, with his head down and his breath blowing out in white clouds in the cool air.

I stood perfectly still, hoping that he would ignore me but his little eyes were fixed on me and my basket. His heavy head started to sweep from side to side, and his fore leg began to pore at the ground. He was not amused at this invasion of his territory. For all I knew he also liked mushrooms, and I was in considerable danger, and very scared.

I had a healthy respect for bulls, but the gate to the field was a hundred yards away, and there was no way though the hedge, which was six feet high and bristling with intermeshed thorns. Both dogs were beside me and suddenly both took off, straight towards the bull, barking as they went. As they reached him, and he swung his horns towards them, they separated and circled round him, distracting him, and I sidled towards the gate, anxious not to attract his attention.

Again and again the dogs raced round the bull, drawing him away from me, and as soon as his back was turned, I took to my heels and fled pell mell for the gate and safety. Once over and with the steel barrier firmly between me and the bull I whistled and the dogs came racing across. Zariah jumped the five barred gate and came up proudly wagging her tail, and Freckles shot through the bottom struts and joined us, equally pleased with herself. By this time the bull was nearing the gate, but as soon as we were out of his field, he lost interest in us, and wandered away grazing as he went.

The mushrooms were delicious, but after that I left that field alone, or joined the gypsies on the golf course in the early morning.

A path ran from our garden into the woods, and our twelve Aylesbury ducks used to wander freely back and forth, nibbling away at tasty morsels on the ground as they went. They never went very far, but this was an enormous worry to Zariah, who spent her time trying to round them up, and herd them back towards the house.

If they were not around at dusk, we used to go looking for them, and this was the highlight of Zariah's day. Off she would go, and a minute or two later there would be a solitary bark as she found them. A whistle from me, and she would start to drive them home, circling triumphantly around them as they waddled and quacked their way slowly back to base. They had a stoutly built duck house to protect them against the dangers of the night, and those expert grabbers of birds, the fox or the wild cat.

The other experts at animal grab are of course poachers, and I used to see them on moonlit nights moving quietly down the edge of the trees, with sacks over their shoulders. Sometimes I would find a bicycle hidden in the bushes, or there would be the noise of a van pulling away. Pheasants were the main prize, but rabbits also made them a tasty meal, and these were usually stuffed down special pockets in their trouser legs.

In Scotland, I used to hear about the salmon poachers, but the only fishing near the farm was done by the herons, who were expert anglers, and would stand for hours absolutely still, as if carved from grey stone, waiting for a strike. Very little escaped their stabbing beaks, and I never knew one to miss.

For two months one summer when we had surplus grazing, we had thirty sheep on the fields, and these caused more trouble than all the horses put together. Most of them were white, but their leader was black faced and as canny as could be. For three days after they arrived, all was well, and I gazed at them cheerfully, and thought how peaceful keeping a shepherd's life must be.

The fourth day after their arrival was hot, and the sun beat down upon the pastures. As I looked out over the idyllic scene, I realised that the whole herd had vanished. Round the fields I went, and at the bottom of the far field, down by the stream, I saw a heron fly up. When I got there there was a gap under a fence, and the whole lot had meandered onto a nearby field. It took me twenty minutes to get them back, and another ten to block the escape route, and the following day the same thing happened.

I must have run miles, seething with fury. Once I was actually checking them from the top of the hill, when I saw their rascally leader digging into the bank beneath a hedge. Before I could reach him, he had his head and shoulders through the hole, and was pushing and shoving with all his considerable weight to enlarge it. By the time I got down the slope, he was away, followed by half a dozen of his stupid companions.

It took me ages to retrieve them, and I grew to hate that black faced woolly villain with a deadly hatred. After six weeks I could stand it no longer, and sent for their owner to collect them. He arrived with a large lorry, and two sheep dogs, and stood leaning against the bonnet while the dogs rounded them up with effortless ease.

Those sheep caused me more trouble than all the rabbits, hens, ducks or horses that I have had to chase after, and I have a healthy respect for shepherds. They lead a tough life.

Chapter 22

"The Changing Year"

Every season had its own beauty at the farm. As the frozen earth of winter thawed out, everywhere became alive with the sound of running water. The stream turned into a river, and threatened to wash away the bridge over the track, and the front paddock became waterlogged, with shining pools lying on the surface of the clay soil.

Great clouds of birds then descended on the front paddock. On one side of the field white terns sat in rows on the fence posts, before settling down to communal worm hunts in the wet ground. On the opposite drier half of the field the black crows gathered, so that the area seemed like one vast game of chess, with birds as the pawns. Gulls of all kinds swooped overhead and groups of wading birds with their long beaks and jerky steps stabbed at the muddy pools.

In March as the ground dried out, the wild hares would race over the meadows and across the track. Sometimes they would stop suddenly and sit perfectly still, like grey statues against the grass. Then they would leap straight up into the air, and dance around shadow boxing before racing on as if they had urgent business a hundred miles away.

At this time of year they were fearless. They

would run along the road kinking and dodging as if following an unseen path, completely oblivious of any traffic or person who happened to be near. We were irrelevant to their world, and our plodding steps were so slow that to them we were invisible. They were alive and part of the green burst of Spring, with every quivering whisker and antennae tuned to the universe.

In late April, weeks later than in the warm South, came the daffodils, and the front garden of the steading turned into a carpet of deep purple crocus and soft white banks of perennial candytuft.

The pasture began to grow and the horses became desperate to go out, snatching odd mouthfuls of grass at every opportunity. To them hay had lost its winter charm, and the spring grass drew them like a magnet.

This was the time of year when little ponies were at risk. Left to themselves they would gorge until they became circular and their overburdened feet would swell from the rich diet. The worst pastures had to be kept for the fattest ponies, much to their disgust, and the horses became as high as kites on the rich new growth.

Each year a covey of partridge chicks would scuttle along the hedgerows, led by an ever anxious hen, who seemed to be in a permanent state of flap. She was always trying to round them up, and as they scattered in every direction, her head would bob up and down in agitation as she tried to keep count of her wayward brood. Usually she had about a dozen chicks, and most years seven or more would survive to the following winter.

A couple of grouse stayed for several seasons, and had a habit of exploding out in a whirl of thrashing wings just as the horses were passing by. The older geldings took no notice but the younger ones would shy and try to bolt, which was most unsettling to a nervous rider. The foals would whirl away in fright and then gallop off lost in the sheer joy of speed and movement, while Amber would lumber along behind with a harassed expression, and stomach swinging as she went.

After the rainstorms of April, wild geese would fly over and wheel down in great white swathes to settle on the young corn on the opposite hill. If left undisturbed they would strip the young seedlings bare, but at the sound of a shot, they would rise up in a snow drift of beating wings, circle once or twice and then head away, calling to each other as they flew.

As the earth grew warmer, buttercups edged the fields and the ox- eye daisies pushed up through the grass. Purple vetch and kingcups appeared by the streams, and the willow branches provided grateful shade for the ponies, as they stood up to their fetlocks in the cool water, their tails continually swishing back and forth against the flies.

This was the time when many farmers were growing oil seed rape, and its heavy fetid scent filled the air as the bees swarmed on the blossoms. The nearby slopes were brilliant with the yellow blooms and when you had bright chestnut horses on green pasture below, and the purple scented lilac trees that edged the garden framing the scene, you felt as if you were living inside a technicolour paintbox.

The colours were as vibrant as the beginning of the world, and your eyes ached from watching, until you needed to wear dark glasses every time you went out.

At the end of April the horses were taken off the big hay field and it was left to grow tall and lush. As the dogs raced through it all that could be seen was a ripple of movement through the seed heads above their running feet.

Then in August came the harvest. Everywhere there was the sound of threshers and heavy farm machinery, and after careful consultation of the weather forecasts, a local farmer would cut our grass and rake it into long lines of sweet smelling hay to dry. As the sap evaporated in the sun, so the hay was turned and shaken, before being baled and stacked in square blocks, which stood like miniature castles dotted about the pasture.

Every morning we would look out anxiously to see if rainstorms were on the way, as if there were a downpour at this stage the hay crop could be either lost or damaged. It was a nervous time for us until the bales were safely stacked, as then any rain would cause less damage. Ideally we needed a dry two weeks, so that we could transfer the new bales to the hay loft without waiting for them to dry out again.

If hay is stored when wet, it gets hotter and hotter until in some cases it can catch fire from internal combustion, and the heat given off from newly stacked bales is high. On the other hand this heat helps the drying process, and makes the hay sweet, and a bale can lose a third of its weight in the first month of storage.

You have to leave pathways and air channels in a hayloft to prevent the green hay overheating and to let the cool air circulate among the bales, and each morning the new hay has to be checked. Sometimes the sides of the bales were almost too hot to touch and if necessary they had to be moved around to let the cooling draughts through. The hay loft was also a happy hunting ground for the farm cats, who found it an ideal place to hide litters of kittens, and spent their days chasing field mice and beetles through the cracks and alleyways and playing follow my leader among the stacks.

Hay making is very hard work, even when machines do the main part for you, and of course everyone is hiring machinery at the same time, and praying for fine weather and combine harvesters which do not break down at the wrong moment. Farmers rush around with an oil can in one pocket and a screwdriver and baling twine in the other, and keep one eye on the barometer.

We were also lent a conveyor belt by a next door farmer, which helped considerably, as we had no machinery of our own, and when the hay was being transferred to the lofts, everyone, even the reluctant passer by was roped in to help.

One stiflingly hot day, we were stacking hay and transferring it from the trailer to the loft twelve feet up. Six of us were all working against time as the atmosphere was heavy and there was the odd roll of thunder in the distance. Half the crop was being stored at the farm, and the rest sold or stored elsewhere as part payment for the farmer's expertise, and that year the weather had been good, so that the hay bales were heavier than usual and harder to handle.

By the time the hay was safely inside, our arms felt like lead, and we were covered in small scratches. We were itching from insect bites and melting from the heat, but we were happy. Everyone sat peacefully in a row on top of the trailer, and watched the storm clouds build up on the horizon. Our hands clasped ice cold cans of beer, while our hair was full of hay seeds and our minds empty of thought. I felt as if my muscles had seized up for ever and I never wanted to move again.

Into this tranquil scene came a distant clatter as a black car turned off the road into the track. It chugged slowly towards us and came to a grinding halt by the side of the barn. The farmer opened one eye and gazed warily down. The car door opened and the farmer's mother stepped out armed with sandwiches, a smile and a vast brown thermos, and at the same moment six hands clutching six beer cans shot behind six backs.

"I brought you some lemonade," she called up cheerfully, and passed up the thermos, "and some food to keep you going. You need something cool this weather!"

Once the hay was safely stored and the harvest over, the September weather turned misty and damp, and the white caps of mushrooms sprouted overnight. Three of the fields grew these in great abundance, and for weeks we had vast breakfasts of mushrooms fresh picked from the field. Each morning I would collect bowls full of these

"I brought you some nice cold lemonade!"

delicacies, and visitors would have pounds pressed upon them as they left.

The ponies liked them as well, especially Janie, and she used to get most indignant if her particular patch was raided, and would rush over and start munching as soon as she saw me approaching. I have never tasted mushrooms like them, but then they were cooked almost before the dew was dry on their firm white skins, and with bacon and eggs they were a gourmet's delight.

As the clouds built up the mists would melt away and the weather would break in a roar of autumn storms. The trees turned and shed their leaves, and every morning the wind currents drove them in a great pile into the car port where they could be easily gathered up. With our supply of hay safely stacked above and the straw for bedding stacked below we were prepared for the winter, and as the days grew shorter I filled up the deep freezers and laid in supplies of bagged feed for the horses.

Each autumn I gathered the blackberries that hung in heavy black bunches from the hedgerows, and made wine. Sometimes I made elder and rosehip as well, but blackberry was the favourite, as it had a kick like a mule, and the rich flavour of a claret. The demi-johns stood in rows in the under stair cupboard, with their air locks popping away, and the heady smell of raw wine wafting out whenever the door was opened.

At the same time the starlings used to meet up together in the ash tree at the edge of the yard. Every evening they murmured and argued with each other, and more and more joined them until there must have been a thousand or more on the laden branches, and their twittering and song would grow louder and louder until you couldn't hear yourself speak. This would go on till dusk, when they would suddenly all fall silent, before rising up like a swarm of bees against the sunset sky, and vanishing over the hill.

As the days grew shorter, the goodness went out of the pasture, and the horses had to be fed extra hay and bucket feeds. The nights turned colder and the first frosts came only to give way to a brief spell of Indian summer.

This was my favourite season of the year, when the leaves turned orange and tawny and brown, full of warm lion colours that dressed the hillsides, before the cold winds stripped the trees down to their bones, and their skeleton branches stood out stark against the snow clouds of winter.

As the ground started to freeze, and the hills grew bleak, so the life of the farm closed in on itself. Riding lessons, if any, had to take place in the school, and trekking ceased as the visitors grew fewer. Life moved at a slower pace as if the whole world slept and we waited for the return of Spring.